Henry Blackburn, Randolph Caldecott

Breton Folk

An Artistic Tour in Brittany

Henry Blackburn, Randolph Caldecott

Breton Folk
An Artistic Tour in Brittany

ISBN/EAN: 9783744768795

Printed in Europe, USA, Canada, Australia, Japan

Cover: Foto ©ninafisch / pixelio.de

More available books at **www.hansebooks.com**

CAVALIERS AND ROUNDHEAD.

(See page 101)

Breton Folk

AN ARTISTIC TOUR IN BRITTANY

BY

HENRY BLACKBURN.

WITH ONE HUNDRED AND SEVENTY ILLUSTRATIONS BY

R. CALDECOTT.

BOSTON.
JAMES R. OSGOOD AND COMPANY
1881

PREFACE.

The following notes were made during three summer tours in Brittany, in two of which the Author was accompanied by the Artist.

Breton Folk is not a description of the antiquities of Brittany, nor even a book of folk-lore. It is a series of sketches of a "black-and-white country" under its summer aspect; of a sombre land shrouded with white clouds, peopled with peasants in dark costumes, wide white collars and caps, black and white cattle and magpies.

The illustrations, one hundred and seventy in number, have been drawn by the Artist from sketches made on the spot, and, apart from their artistic qualities, have the curious merit of truth. They have been engraved with the utmost care by Mr. J. D. Cooper.

CONTENTS.

LIST OF ILLUSTRATIONS.

CHAPTER III.

CHAPTER IV.

CHAPTER V.

CHAPTER IX.

CHAPTER X.

CHAPTER XIII.

|---|---|---|
Caps of Morbihan ...		190
Vannes from the River ...	*face*	190
An Old Inn		192
In a Café...		193
Three Hot Men of Vannes		194
Side-spring Boots ...		195
Some Inhabitants ...		198
A Chase		200

BRETON FOLK:

AN ARTISTIC TOUR IN BRITTANY

CHAPTER I.

THE WESTERN WING.

I N an old-fashioned country-house there is often to be found a room
built out from the rest of the structure, forming, as it were, the
extreme western wing. It has windows looking to the west, its door
of communication with the great house, and, in summer-time, a southern
exterior wall laden with fruit and fragrant with clematis, honeysuckle,
or jasmine. The interior differs from the rest of the mansion both in

B

its furnishing and in the habits of its occupants.   It is a room in which
there is an absence of bright colours, where everything is quiet in tone
and more or less harmonious in aspect; where solid woodwork takes
the place of gilding, where furniture is made simply and solidly for
use and ease, where decoration is *the work of the hand*—holding a
needle, a chisel, or a hammer.   The prevailing colours in this quaint
old room, which give a sense of repose on coming from more highly
decorated saloons, are blue, grey, and green—the blue of old china, the
grey of a landscape by Millet or Corot, the green that we may see
sometimes in the works of Paul Veronese.

This "western wing" is haunted, and full of mysteries and legends;
its furniture is antique, and has seldom been dusted or put in order.
Nearly every object is a curiosity in some way, and was designed in a
past age; on the high wooden shelves over the open fireplace there are
objects in wrought metal work, antique-shaped pots and jars   About
the room are fragments of Druidical monuments, menhirs and dolmens
of almost fabulous antiquity, ancient stone crosses, calvaries, and carvings,
piled together in disorderly fashion, with odd-shaped pipes, snuffboxes,
fishing-rods, guns, and the like; on the walls are small, elaborate,
paintings of mediæval saints in roughly carved gilt frames, and a few
low-toned landscapes by painters of France; on shelves and in niches
are large brown volumes with antique clasps, and perhaps a model in
clay of an old woman in a high cap, a priest, or a child in sabots.

The room is a snuggery, well furnished with pipes and tobacco, and
hitherto evidently not much visited by ladies; but the door is open wide
to the rest of the mansion, through which the strains of Meyerbeer's
opera of *Dinorah* may sometimes be heard.   The lady visitor is welcome
to this out-of-the-way corner, but she must not be surprised to find herself greeted on entering in a language which, with all her knowledge of
French, she can scarcely understand; to be asked, perhaps, to take a
pinch of snuff, and to conform in other homely ways to the habits of the
inhabitants.

Such a quiet, unobtrusive corner—pleasant with its open windows
to the summer air, but much blown and rained upon by winter storms—

is Brittany, the "western wing" of France, holding much the same position geographically and socially to the rest of the country, as the room we have pictured in the great house, to the rest of the mansion.

The Brittany described in these pages is comprised principally of the three departments of CÔTES-DU-NORD, FINISTÈRE, and MORBIHAN, the inhabitants of these districts standing apart, as it were, from the rest of France, preserving their own customs and traditions, speaking their own language, singing their own songs, and dancing their own dances in the streets in 1879. In these three departments is comprehended nearly all that is most characteristic of the Bretons, and the district forms itself naturally into a convenient summer tour of three or four weeks.

Brittany is essentially the land of the painter. It would be strange indeed if a country sprinkled with white caps, and set thickly in summer with the brightest blossoms of the fields, should not attract artists in search of picturesque costume and scenes of pastoral life. Rougher and wilder than Normandy, more thinly populated, and less visited by the tourists, Brittany offers better opportunities for outdoor study, and more suggestive scenes for the painter. Nowhere in France are there finer peasantry ; nowhere do we see more dignity of aspect in field labour, more nobility of feature amongst men and women ; nowhere more picturesque ruins ; nowhere such primitive habitations and, it must be added, such dirt. Brittany is still behindhand in civilisation, the land is only half cultivated and divided into small holdings, and the fields are strewn with Druidical stones. From the dark recesses of the Montagnes Noires the streams come down between deep ravines as wild and bare of cultivation as the moors of Scotland, but the hillsides are clothed thickly in summer with ferns, broom, and heather. Follow one of these streams in its windings towards the sea, where the troubled waters rest in the shade of overhanging trees, by pastures and cultivated lands, and we may see the Breton peasants at their "gathering-in," reaping and carrying their small harvest of corn and rye, oats and buckwheat ; the women with white caps and wide collars, short dark skirts, and heavy wooden sabots, the men in white woollen jackets, breeks (*bragous bras*), and black gaiters,

broad-brimmed hats and long hair streaming in the wind—leading oxen
yoked to heavy carts painted blue. Here we are reminded at once of
the French painters of pastoral life, of Jules Breton, Millet, Troyon, and
Rosa Bonheur; and as we see the dark brown harvest fields, with the
white clouds lying low on the horizon, and the strong, erect figures and
grand faces of the peasants lighted by the evening sun, we understand
why Brittany is a chosen land for the painter of *paysages*. Low in tone
the landscape is, sombre as are the costumes of the people, cloudy
and fitful in light and shade as is all this wind-blown land, there is yet a
clearness in the atmosphere which brings out the features of the country
with great distinctness, and impresses them upon the mind.

To the antiquary who knows the country, and is perchance on the
track of a newly discovered menhir, long buried in the sands; to the
poet who would seek out and see that mystic island of Avilion,

> "Where falls not hail, or rain, or any snow,
> Nor ever wind blows loudly";

to the historian who would add yet other links in the chain of facts in
the strange eventful history of Brittany; to the resident Englishman and
sportsman, who knows the corners of the trout streams and the best
covers for game, scanty though they be, the tour suggested in these
pages will have little interest; but to the English traveller who
would see what is most characteristic and beautiful in Brittany in a short
time, we should say—

Enter by the port of St. Malo from Southampton (or by Dol, if
coming from France), and take the following route, diverging from it
into the country districts as time and opportunity will permit. From
St. Malo to Dinan by water; from Dinan to Lamballe by diligence (or
railway), thence to St. Brieuc, Guingamp, Lannion, Morlaix, Brest,
Quimper, Quimperlé, Hennebont, Auray, Vannes, and Rennes.

Thus, then, having set the modern tourist on his way, and provided
for the exigencies of rapid holiday-making, let us recommend him to
diverge from the beaten track as much as possible, striking out in every
direction from the main line of route, both inland and to the coast,

travelling *by road* as much as possible, and seeing the people, as they
are only to be seen, "off the line."

In *Breton Folk* the reader will be troubled little with the history
of Brittany, with the wars of the Plantagenets, or with the merits
of various styles of architecture, but some general impression of the
country may be gathered from its pages, and especially of the people
as they are to be seen to-day.

CHAPTER II.

St. Malo -- St. Servan — Dinard -- Dinan.

ON a bright summer's morning in July the *ballon captif*, which we may use in imagination in these pages— our French friends having taught us its use in peace as well as in war—floats over the blue water-gate of Brittany like a golden ball. The sun is high, and the tide is flowing fast round the dark rock islands that lie at our feet, pouring into the harbour of St. Malo, floating the vessels and fishing-boats innumerable that line the quays inside the narrow neck of land called Le Sillon, which connects the city with the mainland, and driving gay parties of bathers up the sands of the beautiful Baie d'Écluse at Dinard.

On the map on the opposite page, we see the relative positions of St. Malo, St. Servan, and Dinard also the mouth of the river Rance, which flows southward, wide and strong, into innumerable bays, until it winds under the walls and towers of Dinan. Looking down upon the city, now alive with the life which the rising tide gives to every sea-port; seeing the strength of its position seaward, and the protection from without to the little forests of masts, whose leaves are the bright trade banners of many nations, it is easy to understand how centuries ago St. Malo and St. Servan were chosen as military strongholds,* and

---

* St. Servan is built on the site of Aleth, one of the six capitals of ancient Armorica; there was a monastery here in the sixth century.

how in these later times St. Malo has a maritime importance apparently out of proportion to its trade, and to its population of not more than 14,000 inhabitants.

From a bird's-eye point of view we may obtain a clearer idea of St. Malo and its neighbourhood than many who have actually visited these places, and can judge for ourselves of its probable attractions for a summer visit. It seems unusually bright and pleasant this morning, for the light west wind has cleared the air, and carried the odours of St. Malo landward. There is to be a regatta in the afternoon, the principal course being across, and across, the mouth of the Rance, between St. Malo and Dinard, and already little white sails may be seen spread in various directions, darting in and out between the rock islands outside the bay. On one of these islands, Grand Bé, marked with a cross on the map, is the tomb of the illustrious Châteaubriand, a plain

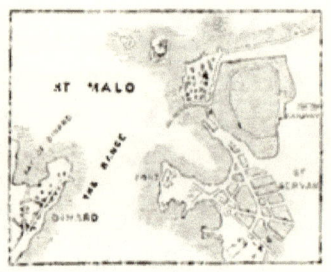

granite slab, surmounted by a cross, and railed in with a very ordinary-looking iron railing. This gravestone, which stands upon an eminence, and is conspicuous rather than solitary, is described by a French writer as a romantic resting-place for the departed diplomatist, characteristic and sublime—" ni arbres, ni fleurs, ni inscription—le roc, la mer et l'immensité"; but as a matter of fact it is anything but solitary in summer-time, and it is more visited by tourists than sea-gulls. The waves are beating round it now, but at low water there will be a line of pedestrians crossing the sands: some to bathe and some to place *immortelles* on the tomb.

The sands of Le Sillon are covered with bathers and holiday crowds in dazzling costumes, the rising tide driving them up closer to the rocks every minute. Everywhere there is life and movement; the narrow, winding streets of St. Malo pour out their contents on the seashore; little steamers pass to and from Dinard continually, fishing and pilot

boats come and go, and yachts are fluttering their white sails far out
at sea. Everything looks gay, for the sun is bright, and it is the day
of the regatta.

Looking landward, the eye ranges over a district of flat, marshy land,
that once was sea, and we may discern in the direction of Dol an island
rock in the midst of a marshy plain, at least three miles from the sea.
On the summit of this rock is a chapel to Notre Dame de l'Espérance,
and near it, standing alone on the plain, is a column of grey granite
nearly thirty feet high, one of the "menhirs" or "Druid stones" that
we shall see often in Brittany. Eastward there is the beautiful bay of
Cancale, famous for its oyster-fisheries; the village built on the heights
is glistening in the sunlight, and the blue bay stretches away east and
north as far as Granville. Cancale is also crowded this morning, for
it is the fashion to come from St. Malo on fête days, to eat oysters, and
to *pay* for them. A summer correspondent, who followed the fashion,
writes: "The people of Cancale are amongst the most able and
industrious fishermen in Brittany, and the oysters from the parcs of
Cancale are famous even in the Parisian restaurants; but in the cabarets
of Cancale the charges resemble those of Paris." We mention this by
the way because travellers who have taken up their quarters at the
principal hotels at St. Malo, finding the charges higher than they
expected, might, without a caution, take wing to Cancale. They may
be attracted thither, for the day at least, to see the fishing operations,
to study costume, to explore the coast by boat, or to visit the island
monastery of St. Michel. The water is smooth in the shallow bay
of Cancale, and the view extending over miles of blue sea to the
green hills beyond Avranches makes a charming picture.

The aspect of St. Malo from the sea is that of a crowd of grey houses
with high-pitched roofs, surrounded with stone walls and sixteenth-
century towers, and with one church spire conspicuous in the centre. At
high-water the waves beat up against the granite rocks and battlements,
and St. Malo seems an island; at low water it stands high on a
pediment of granite, surrounded by little island rocks and wide plains of
sand; the spring tides rising nearly forty feet above low-water mark,

But the chief interest of St. Malo is undoubtedly outside of it. In the narrow, tortuous streets, shut in by high walls, we experience something of the sensation of dwellers in modern Gothic villas ; we have insufficient light and air, we are cramped for space, but we know at the same time that, outwardly, we are extremely picturesque. "Rien de triste et de provinciale comme la ville de Saint-Malo, où tout le monde est couché à 9 h. du soir ; rues noires et tortueuses ; pas de soleil, ni de mouvement ; enfin une ville morte." Such is the popular French view of it in the height of the season, when prices at the hotels are nearly as high as in Paris.

The fortifications and towers of St. Malo are interesting as examples of military architecture of the sixteenth century ; the castle with its four round towers was erected, it is said, by Queen-Duchess Anne to assert her power over the bishops of St. Malo, who had held it from the time when it was an island monastery. From the ramparts and quays we can best see many of the old houses and residences of the wealthy traders of the last century, now dilapidated or turned into barracks or public offices ; and we may also note here and there, in narrow streets, remnants of carved timber beams and wooden pillars which formed the frontage of some of the oldest houses. We can walk upon the ramparts all round the town, from which there are extensive views over sea and land ; and we can inhale, on the western side, the fresh breezes of the sea, and, on the other, the odours rising from innumerable unwashed streets and alleys. The church, the spire of which was completed by order of Napoleon III., has little architectural interest. The structure dates from the twelfth century, but its present aspect is modern and tawdry, with a huge high-altar, candlesticks, gilt furniture, relics, and artificial flowers. The most noteworthy objects are some carved woodwork in the chancel, and a stained-glass window.

The principal streets of St. Malo are modernised, and the shops are full of wares from Paris and Rennes. The appearance and manners of the people are French rather than Breton, and—although the strange patterns of the white caps worn by the peasants and fisherwomen, and the curiously uncouth intonation of voices which already greets our ears, remind us that we are very far from the capital of France—there is little here of distinctive Breton costume.

St. Malo from its position is an important maritime station. It is busy, and busier every year, with shipbuilding, for it has a large fishing population and an export trade with all parts of the world. Brittany is a food-producing land, and St. Malo is its principal northern port ; but its manufactures are comparatively unimportant, and its retail trade is largely dependent on the influx of visitors.

In the suburb of ST. SERVAN, where a few English people live quietly, there is less appearance of commercial activity than in St. Malo. It is in fact a faubourg, comparatively unprotected by walls, and undisturbed by much traffic. Its population of 12,000 have their principal business in St. Malo, and there is a constant stream of pedestrians passing to and fro, crossing on a movable bridge worked by steam, the supports of which are on rails under water. The principal street of St. Servan is wider than Wardour Street in London, but it resembles it somewhat in dinginess, and in the fact that its shops are full of tempting baits for the *bric-à-brac* hunter ; old wood carvings, pots, and stones, which should be purchased with caution.

The Bretons, both in St. Malo and St. Servan, are a little demoralised in summer, and wish to be "fine." To-day being a fête day, they are *en grande toilette*, and the wonderful white caps worn by some of the women are trimmed with real old lace. In the shops and on the promenades the majority of women are dressed as in Paris, and they wear kid gloves "like their betters"; the country people and the fishing and poorer class of Malouins, only, wearing any distinctive costume. The fishermen of Cancale make money and save it, and send their children to school by train to Rennes, and the fisherman's daughter comes back in a costume that makes her neighbours envious. Every year more white caps are thrown aside, for Mathilde will not be outdone by Louise ; and so the change goes on, and each year the markets of St. Malo and St. Servan have less individuality of costume.

Nevertheless, groups such as are sketched are to be seen to-day in St. Malo, St. Servan, and Dinard : the women in white caps, dark stuff gowns, and neatly made shoes; the men in blue serge and sabots The women's caps vary in pattern according to their district. They generally wear a close-fitting under cap, with a small high-crimped crown, and a wide lappet pinned on the top of the head. In St. Malo

we may see Normandy as well as Brittany caps, and it is not until we get farther into the interior that the costume of the district is strongly marked.*

* The caps peculiar to different parts of Brittany are indicated at the head of each chapter.

DINARD—once a little fishing-village, now a fashionable watering-place—the position of which we see on the map on page 7, is a delightful residence in summer, and nearly as dear as Trouville, in Normandy : but the air is bracing and exceptionally good, the walks in the neighbourhood shady and delightful, and the bathing in the sheltered Baie d'Écluse as good as any in France. In Dinard there are about 800 houses and villas in pleasant gardens, most of which are let for a short summer season of three months. There is a well managed " Établissement des Bains " and casino, and several good hotels. Dinard is the starting-point to reach Dinan by road ; also for the little fishing-villages of St. Briac and St. Jacut, on the coast westward. At St. Briac the visitor who does not care to be fashionable will find an inn, good bathing, and summer quarters of a rougher kind than at Dinard ; and at St. Jacut there is a convent standing almost out at sea, where the nuns take boarders in summer for a very small sum. At Dinard you play at croquet on the sands ; at St. Briac you scramble over granite rocks, and fish in the pools under their shadows ; at St. Jacut you wander over the sands with a shrimp-net, and in the evening help the nuns to draw water from the convent well.

But we have come to Brittany to sketch and to note what is most characteristic and picturesque. So far, on the threshold as it were, what have we seen ? Coming from England, and sailing southward into its blue bay on a summer morning, there was an impression of brightness and colour unusual on our own shores. In St. Malo itself three pictures remain upon the memory. The first is the sunset between the islands and across the sands, near the bathing-place of Le Sillon ; the second the moonlight view of its cathedral tower at the end of a narrow street, filling it and towering above it with a grandeur of effect almost equal to that of St. Stephen's at Vienna ; the third picture is in the small courtyard of the Hôtel de France. This house, or part of it, belonged to the family of the Vicomte de Châteaubriand, and it was here, in a room facing the sea, that the celebrated author and diplomatist was born. In the hotel the family arms (the peacock's plume) are emblazoned, and just outside its gates, in the little dusty square called

La Place de Châteaubriand," a new bronze statue, bright and shining, has lately been erected to his memory. Travellers imprisoned between the narrow streets and dingy walls of St. Malo, fortified and barricaded against the fresh breezes of the sea, may perchance seek the cool courtyard of the Hôtel de France as a place of refuge during the heat of the day, and, if not quite tired of hearing of Châteaubriand, may dwell in imagination upon the historic associations of this house. In a corner of the courtyard, now used as a café, there is an old stone staircase leading to the first *étage*, such as we may see in the court-yard of many a French château, and upon it there lingers this afternoon an English girl in the costume most affected by society in 1878. She wears a rich, dark, close-fitting dress in simple folds, spreading where it trails upon the rough granite steps with the stealthy grandeur of a peacock's tail upon a ruined wall. As she turns her head and leans over between the pillars of the covered balcony, her " Rubens hat " and fair hair are framed in antique carved stone. The effect is accidental, but the harmonious combination of costume and architecture brings out suddenly the beauties of each, and gives us a glimpse, not to be forgotten, of the graces of a past age.

THE RANCE.

The tide is now flowing fast up the Rance, filling its numerous bays and inlets, floating odd-shaped little boats and rafts that are moored off the villages on its banks, running up here and there inland between rocks and trees and forming miniature lakes, which will disappear as the tide goes down. The little steamer for Dinan starts from the Quai Napoléon, and goes up on the flood in about three hours, having just time to reach Dinan and return to St. Malo before the water has subsided. The foredeck is crowded with market-women and small merchandise, and on the afterdeck, which is but a few yards square, there are some French and English tourists under a canvas awning, which is useful alike for shelter from sun, rain, or cinders. Steering south-east by south, we steam gently up the Rance, getting a fine

view of St. Servan in passing (a view which we should have missed
altogether by the land route to Dinan); a river that, near its mouth,
seems to have no boundaries or banks, that flows in and out amongst
cultivated fields, then suddenly through narrow defiles of rocks and
under the shadow of forest trees that might be Switzerland. Once
or twice we sail, as it were, in an inland lake, or, as the French call
it, "une petite Méditerranée"; we can neither see where we entered
nor any outlet on our route. There are fishing and market boats,
lying in quiet corners, and one or two pleasure yachts with flags flying,
moored in the prettiest spots near modern summer châlets, the
slate roofs of which appear above the trees. We pass one considerable village, St. Suliac, on the east bank, behind which is the ancient
fort of Châteauneuf; and, on the west, the grey walls of more than
one old château are visible. The water is blue and tidal until we
arrive at a lock a few miles from Dinan, when the little steamer
ploughs through a narrow canal-like stream, and sends the water
flowing over the banks, washing the stems of the poplar trees.

We are entering Brittany now, and are far out of hearing of the
waves that beat upon St. Malo, and of the band of the casino on its
sands. On either side the valleys are rich with verdure and with
orchards of fruit. There are farmhouses and villas dotted about, and
peasants at work in the fields. We pass close to the banks during
the last mile, and are shut in by rocks and trees; but all at once the
view enlarges, and there rises before us a scene so grand and, at the
same time, so familiar that we feel delighted and rewarded at having
approached Dinan by water. The prevailing tone of landscape during
the last few miles has been sombre, and the valleys in shadow with
their dark granite rocks and gloom of firs have contrasted picturesquely
with the sunshine on distant fields. As we reach Dinan in the
afternoon, the valley of the Rance is in shadow, whilst above and
before us, crowning a hill, are the old roofs, towers, and spires of
Dinan shining in the sun. The sides of the valley here are almost
precipitous, and across it, high above our heads, is a plain modern
viaduct, reaching to the suburb of Lanvallay. Dinan is on the west

or left bank of the Rance; and near the bridge where we land the steep streets of the old town reach to the water's edge. Above our heads are feudal towers, and parts of old walls, and the grey roofs of houses between the trees, and away southward the valley of the

FRUIT STALL AT DINAN.

Rance winding out of sight. We said it was a familiar picture, for the approach to Dinan by water and the view from the hills on the opposite bank of the Rance, seen under summer suns, have been perpetuated in brightness by many an English artist. It is well to see Dinan thus, *en couleur de rose*, and to remember it in its most bright and attractive aspect, for on a nearer and longer acquaintance

our impressions may change.   Dinan—situated on the summit and
slopes of wooded hills, their dark granite sides appearing here and
there through the trees, its mediæval towers and terraces, and its old
grey houses with pointed roofs, and its handsome white modern
houses—forms a good background to the market-women, with their
stalls of fruit and vegetables, peasants in blue blouses, and the
usual summer crowd of tourists, including Parisians in suits of white,
with broad straw hats and blue umbrellas, thronging on the quay
waiting for our little steamer.   There are several hundred English
residents in Dinan, and the voices in the streets have a familiar
sound, neither French nor Breton.   But the population, including
English, scarcely exceeds 10,000 even in summer ; and the inhabitants,
who are not given up to trading with visitors, are principally occupied
in agriculture, or working in their dark dwellings at hand looms.

As we climb up a steep, dirty street, leading from the quay, called
the Rue de Jersual, and under a Gothic gateway—past old houses, with
high-pitched roofs and leaning timbers, rising one above another in
irregular steps—we hear the sound of the loom in the darkness on
either side, and the inhabitants come out to stare as usual ; shining
red faces, under white caps, lean out from little latticed windows and
from doorways, and in the gutters many a little pair of sabots stuffed

with hay is rattling on the stones.   It
is a ladder of cobblestones and dirt, cool
and slippery, sheltered by projecting eaves
from the afternoon sun ; the principal
approach from the river a century ago,
up which a stream of pilgrims files into
the upper town.   They pause to take
breath at the top, and then disperse on
the *Place*, where, in front of dusty rows
of trees, the omnibuses and carts, which
have come round by the broad, circuitous
road, are setting down travellers.   The
entrance to the inn is blocked by a loaded hay cart, stuck fast in the
archway of the house, as in the sketch.   We have ascended at least

300 feet to the *Place*, and take up our quarters in one of the hotels in the wide open square, looking as dusty and uncared for as usual in French provincial towns, and commanding, as usual also, no view of the country round.

In a few minutes the bustle caused by the arrival of travellers has ceased, and the principal square of Dinan resumes its ordinary aspect on a summer's day. Nurses, in white caps, sit knitting under the shadows of stunted trees, while the children play in the dust; cavalry officers of all grades play at cards and drink absinthe at little

tables half hidden by trees planted in boxes at the hotel doors; ladies and children, a priest, a workman in blue blouse dragging a load of stones, a woman coming from market, and an Englishman or two, on pleasure intent, with draggled beard and grey knickerbockers, as is the fashion of the time. Above the trees, the houses across the square rise in irregular lines, their steep roofs, old and sun-stained, are full of variety and colour; behind them tree tops wave, and great masses of white clouds drive northward to the sea.

Dinan is full of interest both for the artist and the antiquary. The cathedral of St. Sauveur, with its fine carved doorway and Romanesque

C

architecture, the old clock-tower in the Rue de l'Horloge, the
mediæval gateways, and the old houses in the narrow streets, form
a succession of pictures worthy of study. It is well to examine
the castle, once occupied by the Queen-Duchess Anne and now a
prison, and to ascend the tower, from which there is a magnificent
view. In the museum at the Mairie there are several interesting
monuments and ecclesiastical relics. And yet perhaps the chief

interest of Dinan is in the variety and beauty of its environs; on
every side will be found charming wooded walks and valleys, from
which we can see its position, set high on green hills, the sky-line a
fringe of trees and towers. The walks on the ramparts, with their
lines of poplars and the views across the deep fosse below will
give an idea of the military architecture of the middle ages, and
especially of the natural strength and importance of Dinan as a
fortified city when besieged by the Duke of Lancaster in 1359 and
defended by the brave Du Guesclin. In St. Malo, Châteaubriand was

the hero; in Dinan it is Du Guesclin, constable of France in the
fourteenth century. In the cathedral of St. Sauveur they have
burned candles before the jewelled casket containing his heart, for
centuries, and on the *Place* there is a poor statue of him in plaster;
but the more lasting monuments are the records of his deeds and the
songs of the people, which we shall hear often on our travels.

Whichever way we turn in Dinan, we find some new view and
point of interest, and the inhabitants are so accustomed to the incursion of strangers, and reap so many benefits by their coming, that
we are allowed to sketch almost undisturbed. There is an old woman
with deformed hands and feet, who sits knitting on the *Place*, whose
familiar figure will be recalled by the sketch on page 21.

The ramparts are comparatively deserted by day, and form a promenade by moonlight worth coming far to see. If ever there was a
spot on earth prepared for lovers, it is surely the broad walk on
the southern ramparts of Dinan, where the moon shines upon the
path between tall waving poplars and silvers the distant trees, where
there is scarcely a sound to break the stillness, where there is room
for every Romeo out of hearing of his neighbour, and where the
sounds of the city are hushed behind granite walls. It is naturally
romantic and beautiful, and, with the associations which cling around its
towers, has a charm which is almost unique; but we must tell the truth.
There are clusters of white roses clinging to the old masonry above,
which have scattered their full-blown leaves at our feet, and below, in
the deep dell which formed the ancient fosse, there is honeysuckle in
the straggling garden; but the odours that rise on the evening air are
not of roses nor of honeysuckle, nor from the broad champaign around.
There surely was never a beautiful spot so defiled. As a picture, the
general aspect of Dinan will remain in memory—a picture not to be
effaced by the erection of large new barracks, or by the railway now
constructing in the valley—stately Dinan with its ancient groves and
terraces, its hanging gardens, and sylvan views.

We must not linger in such a well-known part of Brittany, or we
would take the reader in imagination to one or two of the old

houses in the neighbourhood, like the one sketched below; also, a little way up the river, to the picturesque ruins of the abbey of Lehon. This last is a spot especially to be visited, and where, if we are wise and have time, we should take apartments for a week in summer. Another favourite walk is on the opposite side of Dinan, leaving the town by the ramparts towards the north. Here in the midst of a tangle of briars and bushes, hemmed in on every side, run over with ivy and every variety of creeper, shut off entirely from some points of view by an orchard laden to the ground with fruit and

by a garden of flowers, is the one tower left of the famous château of LA GARAYE. The grey octagonal turret, with its crumbling Renaissance ornament, stands high above the surrounding trees, and catches the evening sunlight long after the avenue of beeches by which it is approached is in gloom. The place is as solemn and quiet, at the end of a long avenue, as any poet could desire; but as we approach the gates of the château of "the lady with the liberal hand," whom Mrs. Norton has immortalised in her poem, there are the usual signs of demoralisation. There are pigs about, and tourists; and the show is charged for in the usual way. We pay our money and take away some souvenir of the place. Americans who have read (and recited often in their own homes)

"The Lady of La Garaye" sometimes make Dinan the extreme
western point of their tour in Europe, and have trodden the ground
into a deep track to the château with their pilgrim feet ; but the position
is inconvenient for tourists who have much to see, and so, it is understood, they are going to buy the turret and take it home. The idea is
not as absurd as it may sound ; it is a very pretty ruin as it stands, but

it will fall soon if not cared for, and the low wall on either side of the
turret will disappear behind the fruitful orchard. The old hospital is
now used as a farmshed, but wants repairing to be habitable ; and the
ancient cider-press, with its massive wooden beams, lies rotting in the
sun. The farm children are gathering blackberries from the bushes
which grow between the hearthstones of the old banquet-hall, poultry
swarm in my lady's boudoir, and there is a hum of bees and insects
about the ruin.

We have said nothing of the English colony and church at Dinan, of the convent of the Ursulines and their good works, or of the people to be seen on market-days, because Dinan is well known to travellers, and there is very little to distinguish it from other French towns. To see the people, and sketch the Bretons in their most picturesque aspects, we must go farther afield.

As we leave Dinan by diligence with much cracking of whips and jingling of bells, through the wide square tenanted as usual by white-capped nurses and idlers; rolling in the high *banquette* down past the old gateways, out into the country road towards the west, we see the last of Dinan and its towers. Whether in its autumn beauty with rich surrounding woods, or with its winter curtain folded softly, with tassels and fringes of frost, Dinan leaves a brilliant impression upon the mind. We forget the modern incursion of tourists, and the

demoralisation amongst the poorer inhabitants caused by the scattering of sous, we forgive its dingy, neglected streets, its ill-kept boulevards and squares, and its slow, unenterprising ways; we remember only its grandeur and picturesqueness.

As we pass out by the Porte de Brest, we meet a Breton *propriétaire* and his wife in a cart, whom we must not take for peasants because of the black stuff gown and white cap of the bright-faced woman, and the broad-brimmed hat and blouse of the man.

We drive through a straggling suburb of houses, where the peasants stare at us from their dark dwellings; we stop at wayside inns— unnecessarily, it would seem—and are surrounded by beggars of all ages and sizes. Here is one who comes suddenly to earth at the sound of wheels, and peers from the darkness of her home underground with the brightness and vivacity of a weasel; her black eyes glisten with astonishment and with the instinct of animal nature scenting food; she transforms herself in an instant from the buoyant youth and almost cherub-like beauty in the sketch to a cringing, whining mendicant. "Quelque chose, quelque chose pour l'amour de Dieu," in good, clear French, nearly all the words that her parents would have her learn, in the intervals of playing and road-scraping—the latter her only serious business in life. But the schoolmaster is abroad in Brittany; the edict has gone forth that every child of France shall henceforth learn the French tongue; and this little creature will be caught and tamed, and civilised into ways that her parents never knew.

One more picture on the road, an incident common enough, but characteristic and worth recording. It is a sultry afternoon, with a deep blue sky and a burning sun. So fierce is the heat that it has silenced for a time the barking of dogs and the arguments of some of our passengers. Just outside a village the straight road, unsheltered even by poplars, is fringed with low brushwood and long grasses withering under a curtain of dust. There is nothing stirring but a little yellowhammer and a magpie on the road, a *cantonnière* in wide straw hat, chipping at a heap of stones, and the lumbering diligence in which we travel; no shelter but in a wood hard by.

Presently we come to a halt in a narrow part of the road, for M. Achille Dufaure's cart of charcoal stops the way. It is a suggestive picture, which we may call "The Hour of Repose." In the foreground, in the burning road, is a tall white charger, encumbered, now in his old age, with a great wooden collar and clumsy harness,

chained to a dark blue cart with dirt-encrusted wheels, half smothered
on this summer's day with a blue woolsack over his shoulders, foaming
at the mouth, and streaming with the wounds of flies and other
injuries, but pricking his ears as of old at the sound of approaching
wheels. In the background, but a few yards off, is a cool wood of
beech and elm, dark in its shadows, green in its depth with ivy and
fern, and fringed against the sky with tops of waving poplars. This
broad mass of green, which comes between the brightness of sky
and the burning road, with its foreground of dry grasses, is relieved

on one spot by a cool ripple of blue—it is Achille lying on his
face asleep, his blouse just lifted by a breeze; he will repose for two
or three hours, whilst his horse stands in the sun, and the hot
shadows lengthen from his heels. No amount of shouting on the
part of our driver will waken the sleeper; blessings and curses,
cracking of whips and blowing of horns, are all tried in vain, and
the monotony of our journey is relieved by the diligence being
dragged, as it might have been at first, over the field at the roadside,
and we resume our way.

As we travel westward, the aspect of the land becomes suddenly
changed; it is clouded over and rained upon, and is a sombre

contrast to the former brightness. After the glare of the sun
the senses are grateful for quiet tones; but the sight is strange,
almost mournful. The district is only a few miles from busy towns
and sea-ports, and on the main line of railway from Paris to Brest,
but it is out of the world, and seems, under its cloudy aspect, farther
than ever removed from civilisation; we pass substantial-looking
farmhouses, but the dwellings of the peasants are generally hovels,

with tumble-down mud walls and immovable windows; in their
gardens are dungheaps and stagnant pools of water. We see women
at work in the fields, girls tending cattle, and the men, generally,
looking on.

The distance from Dinan to Lamballe by road is twenty-five miles,
a slow and sleepy journey of about five hours by the direct route; a
journey seldom taken by travellers since the completion of the railway
westward. Everything we pass on the road looks comparatively untidy,
rough, and poor, with the poverty of ignorance and neglect rather than

of means, for the soil, as we approach Lamballe, is rich, and yields
well. The country is really fruitful, but an acre of land is often
divided into twenty different lots, in each of which there are separate
crops of hemp, buckwheat, or potatoes, or they are filled with gorse
for winter fodder for cattle. The hedges are made of mud-banks,
gorse, and ferns, and the gates between them are formed of felled
trees, the stem forming the upper bar, the roots being left as a
counterpoise to lift the gate on its rough, wooden latch.

The rain ceases as we approach Lamballe; the air is fresh with
the wind coming from the bay of St. Brieuc, and as the sky clears,
we obtain, at intervals on the undulating road, views over finely wooded
valleys, with high hedgerows, banked up and planted with elms and
oaks. The chestnut trees, wet with the rain, are rich in colour, and
the fields of buckwheat lighten the landscape again. Another turn
in the road, and we are in evening light, there is open pasture land,
and the cattle are winding home; at another, a farmer is meditating
on his stock in the corner of a field. Thus we pass from one picture
to another, quaint and idyllic, the last reminding us more of Troyon
than of Rosa Bonheur.

CHAPTER III.

IT is half past five o'clock on a summer's morning at LAMBALLE, and the deep-toned bell of Notre Dame resounds through the valley of the Gouessan. The sun is up and gleams upon the roof tops, and upon the heads of the old women who are sitting thus early in the market-place, surrounded with flowers, taking their morning meal of *potage*. It is market morning, and the open square in the centre of the town is filling fast with arrivals from the country. Everything is fresh from the late rains, and the air is laden with the scent of flowers, butter, and milk. On every side carts are unloading, and itinerant vendors are fitting up stalls for the sale of provisions and goods. There are rows of stalls for the sale of cloth stuffs, shoes, and wooden sabots, for pots and pans, and for innumerable trinkets of small value to tempt the peasantry. The shops are opening one by one, displaying less fashionable, if more useful, wares than we have seen at St. Malo and Dinan ; agricultural implements, and all articles for the use and temptation of the country people who come from far to make purchases, bargaining in a rather uncouth tongue, but with a certain dignity and determination of manner which we shall find peculiar to the Bretons. Both buyers and sellers speak in a language apparently half French and half Welsh, and the majority dress in plain, dark, home-spun stuffs, the men with their blouses, the women with their caps, all put on clean for the day. This market-place at Lamballe is a sight, if only to see the fowls and the flowers. It is full of the killed and wounded, bright plumage and delicate leaves; beauty led captive by vigorous hands, hustled out of the market-place by rosy, unsentimental housekeepers; carried heads downwards, both fowls and flowers!

The noise and chattering of a market morning have begun in earnest, but the great bell of Notre Dame resounds above all; two other churches soon join in the concert, and the clatter of sabots over the rough cobblestones up to the church doors adds to the clamour. It is time to follow the people up the streets, almost too steep for wheels, which lead to the great church of Notre Dame, built on the site of the ancient castle of the counts of Penthièvre.

Travellers, especially summer tourists coming from Dinan or Rennes, on their way westward by railway, seeing the beautiful position of this town, with its church above the valley, pause sometimes to consider "whether Lamballe is worth stopping at for a night." As we are writing for all, we may tell them, as we pause to take breath on the ladder of stones which leads to Notre Dame, that the Gothic pile which crowns the hill before them, whose granite walls almost overhang a precipice, and from the rocks of which its pillars and arches seem to spring, is not only full of historic interest, but has a grandeur of effect in the interior which we shall seldom find equalled in Brittany. The original structure was a castle chapel, built early in the sixteenth century, but the present building does not present many special architectural features of interest, excepting the remains of an ancient rood-loft and some stained glass. The building has undergone several periods of restoration down to the present time, when workmen are busy repairing its outer walls. But the interior, on Sundays and fête days, is a picture to be remembered, and is especially full of human interest. The nave is less obstructed with modern ornaments than usual, and there is a quietness about the services which we do not find in larger towns. There are the usual wooden cabinets set against

the side wall with green curtains in place of doors ; in the centre compart-
ment there is a dark object concealed, and on one side the skirt of a
woman's dress peeps from under the curtain ; it is only Marie in a new
gown telling some of her sins. There are several women kneeling on
chairs, dressed in dark green or brown shawls, stuff dresses, and neat
strong shoes ; all heads turn one way as we enter, the old women,
especially, scanning us from head to foot and mentally taking our
measure as they pray. Here, on this summer morning, crowded with
men, women, and children on their knees, their figures just distinguish-
able in the subdued light, the proportions of the lancet arches supported
by clustering pillars, and the stained-glass windows, have a fine effect.

Before leaving Lamballe, a sketch should be made, from the valley, of
the church of Notre Dame, with its surrounding houses, walls and rocks
in evening light. The drawing, if accurate, will be considered exaggerated,
on account of the extraordinarily picturesque and commanding site. The
views from the terraces and old ramparts of Lamballe form an almost
complete panorama of the country round. It is a view of rich cultivated
land, covered with crops of cereals, and cattle grazing in the valleys.
Over all this land the great bell of Lamballe makes itself heard in
company with the whistle of the locomotive which hurries travellers
on to St. Brieuc, a distance of twelve miles westward.

In ST. BRIEUC we find ourselves in a busy city of 15,000 inhabitants,
apparently too much occupied with trade and agriculture to think about
beautifying their houses and streets. There are many narrow, irregular
streets, in which the old houses have been replaced by others generally
modern and mean ; "une vraie ville de rentiers qui aurait besoin d'être
'hausmannisée.'" There is a large square *Place* for the military, and a
market-place near the cathedral, where the old women congregate. St.
Brieuc, as will be seen on the map, is the principal town in the department ; it carries on a large export trade in the produce of the country,
especially in butter and vegetables, for the English and European
markets. Cattle are exported largely from Légué, the actual port,
about two miles off, in the centre of the bay of Brieuc, hidden from
the town by intervening hills.

In the country round and on the hills overlooking the sea, there
are men and women at work in the fields, girls carrying milk
on their heads from the neighbouring farms, and others busy in
the farmyards. The buckwheat harvest has commenced, and the fields
are being robbed of their rich colour; but the scene is bright with

fresh green and yellow mustard, and rich here and there with clover.
The sombre figures are the peasantry with their dark costumes.
Here we feel inclined, for the first time, to stay and sketch, wandering along the coast to the fishing villages on the western shore
of the wide-spreading bay of St. Brieuc, visiting the farms and
homesteads, and making studies of the interiors of dwellings. The

rough, wasteful method of husbandry, the old farmhouses with their one living-room with massive furniture and mud floors, and the simple manners of the peasants, remind us irresistibly of Ireland, whilst the names of people and places and the intonation of voices are altogether Welsh.

Everyone is at work near St. Brieuc in the summer months, every man, woman, and child, in the fields, on the roads, or on the shore; a bright, quick-witted population, accustomed to the inroads of strangers. The inhabitants are superintended in their occupations by some officers of the line, whose regiments are quartered near the town. The soldiers are sprinkled over the streets, and dot the hillsides with colour. The rattle of drums and the smoke of innumerable bad cigars make a lasting impression in this city.

St. Brieuc, or St. Brioc, is the site of a very ancient bishopric, whose chapter was loyal and powerful to the last. Its history is told best in the strength of its cathedral walls, and especially in the ruins of the tower of Cesson, a castle once commanding the entrance to the bay and the approach to St. Brieuc from the sea. There is

little that is remarkable in the churches, and, unless it be some old
overhanging houses near the cathedral, little to sketch in the town
that we shall not find of a better type elsewhere. The business of
nearly everyone at St. Brieuc is to prepare ox hides, tallow, hemp, and
flax to sell stores for the ships that fit out here for the Newfoundland
cod-fisheries, and generally to provide the agricultural population with
the necessaries of civilisation. The town is as noisy as any French
market-town where soldiers are quartered. In the evening come the
carts from the country, and the clatter of sabots over the stones ; at

sundown the regimental drums, at midnight the evacuation of the
cafés, and the songs of warriors going to their rest ; at dawn a market
generally begins under our windows. When do these people find rest ?
The answer comes laconically from the *femme de chambre* at our inn.
" There is the winter for rest "; and there is the French saying,
applicable enough in this land of noises, that we have " l'éternité pour
nous reposer."

In the neighbourhood of St. Brieuc is a picturesque château, part
of which is shown in the sketch ; on the sky-line fringing the roof are
metal figures of horses, men, and dogs, typical of the chase.

There are modern in. vations of high white houses, factories, steam ploughs, plate-glass windows, and smooth pavements to walk on, and the majority of people one meets in St. Brieuc are dressed in modern fashion, but there are odd corners, and very odd old men and women in the by-streets. There is an old woman who sits in the market-place surrounded by earthenware pots, rather disconsolately, for trade is bad; but who, facing the last rays of the setting sun, unconsciously makes a picture which for colour is a delight to the eye; a comfortable old woman in dark blue dress, with dazzling white cap,

bronzed hands and wrinkled face, all aglow under its snowy awning; a background of brown and blue earthenware piled in straw, a distance of dark shadows, and half defined leaning eaves.

St. Brieuc is much visited in the summer for sea bathing. The large buildings near the sea, surrounded by high walls and gardens, are convents or seminaries, where several hundred children are boarded and educated for about £20 a year. In the summer the children give place to adult *pensionnaires*, who come from all parts of France for the bathing season, and the convents are turned into lodging-houses, reaping a good harvest in spite of the apparently moderate terms of five or six francs a day. These *pensionnaires* spread over the cliffs and sands like summer flies, to be discerned sometimes in the distance as in the sketch.

It is at a village on the cliff near Fort Rosalie that we first see men and women winnowing, their arms extended in the breeze, a bright and characteristic scene recorded exactly in the sketch; a picture soon to vanish before patent winnowing-machines and other improvements. Mathurine, one of the party—who has pinned a clean white band of linen over her flowing hair and under-cap, and put on a dark brown embroidered shawl —takes the opportunity, during the mid-day meal of *potage*, to stand for her portrait.

About midway between St. Brieuc and Guingamp, on the north side of the railway, is the quiet little town of Châtelaudren. It is washed and watered by the Leff, the "river of tears," which, coming from the mountains that we see to the south, winds its way through rich valleys, seaward. In its course, and in its time, the Leff has done much havoc in this peaceful valley, inundating and destroying Châtelaudren in 1773, and still occasionally overflowing its banks. To-day it is to the angler a capital trout stream, if he will follow its course southward to the mountains; to the artistic eye it is a sparkling river of light, set in a landscape of green and grey. In the town of Châtelaudren, with its one wide and rather dreary-looking street, there is not much to detain the visitor, but it is a good starting-point from which to explore the country and the Montagnes Noires. The land is thickly cultivated, and well grown with crops almost down to the sea; and on every side in this autumn time there are signs of industry. From the fields we hear voices of women at work; in the farmyards there is the dull thud of the flail and the burr of the winnowing-machine. Across the sloping fields from the sea come sounds of singing and laughter, disconnected and weird sometimes, from being caught up by the wind, then dropped and taken up again.

Eight miles from Châtelaudren, in a green valley watered by the river Trieux, is the quiet old town of GUINGAMP. Its past history, like that of nearly every town in Brittany, has been so eventful that its present normal state may well be calm; but once a year its inhabitants neither work nor repose. In the month of September they hold their annual Fête de St. Loup, and pilgrims come from all parts of Brittany by excursion trains to the famous "Pardon" of Guingamp.

These religious festivals which are held once a year in nearly every town in Brittany, and are generally combined with dancing, fireworks, and other festivities, are the occasion of a great gathering of the people from remote parts of the country; excursion trains bring tourists and pilgrims from all parts of France, and during the week of the fête it is difficult to find a resting-place in Guingamp. The three principal Pardons are generally held at Ste. Anne d'Auray in Morbihan, in July; at Ste. Anne de la Palue in Finistère, in August, and at Guingamp, in September. The Pardon at Guingamp is held on Sunday and Monday, when processions are formed to the shrine of a saint a mile and a half outside the town, indulgences are granted, relics and crosses are distributed, trinkets are blessed, and sermons preached by the bishop of the diocese to the people assembled in the open air. After the services there is a fête in the town, of which the programme on the next page will give the best idea.

The religious aspect of these Pardons, and the gathering of the pilgrims, is sketched in Chapter XII.; we will therefore speak of Guingamp as it is seen every day. Whether it be from the interest

Programme of the Fête at Guingamp at the Time of the " Pardon."

VILLE DE GUINGAMP

—

FÊTE DE St LOUP

PROGRAMME

—

DIMAN DE [ ] LE SES MATIN, DE ONZE HE HES A MIDI

Musique Militaire sur la Place du Centre

A DEUX HEURES APÈS MIDI, CHAQUE JOUR

*DÉPART DU CORTÉGE, MUSIQUE EN TÉTE, POUR
SAINT-LOUP*

A SIX HEURES DU SOIR

RETOUR, EN VILLE, DES DANSEURS ET DE LA MUSIQUE

—

LES DEUX SOIRS, A HUIT HEURES, SUR LA PLACE DU CENTRE

BAL À GRAND ORCHESTRE

BRILLANTE ILLUMINATION

—

À LA FIN DU BAL

EMBRASEMENT DE TOUTE LA PLACE

Aux Feux de Bengale de diverses couleurs (Effets de Jour, Effets d'Incendie)

GRANDE RETRAITE VÉNITIENNE

AUX PYRAMIDES DE LANTERNES ET FEUX DE BENGALE

Illuminations et Décors, par M. Kervella, de Rennes

attaching to the great annual fête, or from reports of the miraculous
cures that have been effected by the patron saint, Guingamp has always
attracted travellers, and has been written of in terms of rapture which
may astonish a visitor when he sees it for the first time.   It is a town of
not more than 8000 inhabitants, with one principal street, which winds

irregularly down like a stream, spreading and overflowing its banks at one
point, in triangular fashion, in what is
called the market-place, then narrowing
again, and working its way through a
suburb of small houses into the great
high-road to Morlaix. It has two monuments—the church of Notre Dame, and
a bronze fountain in the market-place.
The timbered houses are old, and many
of their gables lean ; the cobblestones
in the streets are rough, and the public
square of dust, with withering trees, built
on the old ramparts, looks as dreary as
any we shall see on our travels. But
it is surrounded by green landscape, and
the view from the walks on the ramparts,
seen through the tops of poplars, is of
a green valley with trees and grey roof-
tops, between which winds the river Trieux, slowly turning water-
wheels.

The church was built between the fourteenth and sixteenth centuries,
and represents several styles of architecture—Romanesque, Gothic, and
Renaissance. It was originally founded as a castle chapel, and part of
the structure is as early as the thirteenth century. It has three towers,
the centre one having a spire. The interior is impressive, on account
of the simplicity of arrangement for services and the comparatively
uninterrupted view of the nave and aisles ; an effect more like that
on entering a cathedral in Spain than in France.

Brittany is a land of lasting monuments; and of its buildings it has been well said, "ce que la Normandie modelait dans le tuf, la Basse-Bretagne le ciselait en granit"; but remembering the magnificent churches we have seen in Normandy, we need not detain the reader long in Notre Dame de Guingamp. If we were asked by tourists if the church of Notre Dame at Guingamp was worth going very far to see, we should answer, No. It is only as a picture that it attracts us much. We shall see finer buildings in other parts of Brittany, but nowhere a more characteristic assembly. The most curious feature is a chapel forming the north porch, which is open and close to the street, lighted at night for services, and separated only from the road by a grille. This *portail*, as it is called, forms the chapel of Notre Dame de Halgoet, and is the sacred shrine to which all come at the fête of Guingamp. It is ornamented by rich stone carving and grotesque gurgoyles. The people of Guingamp love the chapel of Notre Dame de Halgoet; it is a retreat for them by day and by night, a place of meeting for old and young, with a perpetual beggars' mart at the door. This north porch with its open grille is a house of call for rich and poor of both sexes, and

placed as it is in the centre of the town, abutting upon the principal street, it forms part of their everyday life to go in and out as they pass by. It is one of the many welcome retreats in France; in a land of perpetual noises and glare, of shrill, uncouth voices and latchless doors, it is the church that gives us peace and shade.

In the centre of Guingamp is its market-place, and in the centre of the market-place is a fountain, consisting of a circular granite basin with a wrought-iron railing. There is a second basin of bronze, supported by

four sea-horses with conventional wings, and a third by four naiads; the central figure is the Virgin, her feet resting on a crescent. This fountain was constructed by an Italian artist, and its waters played for the first time on the night of the annual Pardon, in 1745. The history of Guingamp is not complete without recounting the story of the construction of this fountain; but regarded from a picturesque point of view, the smooth green bronze with its Renaissance ornamentation harmonises neither with the surrounding houses, with their high-pitched roofs and pointed turrets, nor with the towers of Notre Dame. We are more interested with the living groups which furnish the wide market-place in the morning sun.

A few yards from the cathedral, on the opposite side of the street, is the old Hôtel de l'Ouest, where travellers are entertained in rather rough but bountiful fashion.

"Take a little trout or salmon, caught this morning in the Trieux, a little beef, a little mutton, a little veal, some tongue, some omelettes, some pheasant, some fish salad, some sweets, some coffee, and then—stir gently," is the prescription for travellers who stay at the Hôtel de l'Ouest. As this is an average hotel, it may be worth while to state that the bill presented (by the young lady in the sketch) to *three* English travellers, who spent a night and part of a day there, was 12 fr. 80 c.

Excepting at the time of fêtes, Guingamp is almost as quiet and primitive in its ways as in the days of the Black Prince. Our notes of days spent in this city in different years are the most uneventful in our records. On one summer's morning we hear an unusual sound from the great bell of Notre Dame, and find a procession of priests and choristers winding up the principal street, followed by hundreds of the inhabitants. What is the occasion? "The mother of the Maire is dead; she was a bountiful lady, beloved by all, and we are to bury her this morning." And so the inhabitants turn out *en masse*, and march with slow steps, for about half a mile, to the cemetery. It is a dark, silent stream of people, filling the street, and carrying everything slowly before it: the only sounds being the chanting of the choir, and the repetition of prayers. We follow to the cemetery, which is crowded with graves, each headed by little iron or wooden crosses, hung with immortelles. The procession divides and disperses down the narrow paths, a few only of the friends of the deceased standing near the grave.

At one corner of the cemetery is a shabby little wooden building, like a gardener's tool-house, which seems to excite much interest. A girl, with shining bronzed face, in a snow-white cap, holding a little child by the hand, is coming out of the door; we venture to ask the

reason of her visit. "Just to see my father for a minute," is the ready answer.

In a little wooden box, about the size of a small dog kennel, is her father's skull or *chef*, as it is called; he is tumbling over with his friends in other boxes exactly as in the sketch, which, rough as it is, has the grim merit of accuracy. The sight is a common one in Brittany, but it is startling and takes us by surprise at first, to see at least fifty of these shabby boxes, some on shelves in rows, but generally piled up in disorder and neglect. The lady who is being buried so solemnly this morning will some day be unearthed, and her *chef*, in a box duly labelled and decorated with immortelles, will take its place in the ossuary of Guingamp.

From the high ground near the cemetery, and especially from a hill a little farther from the town in a north-easterly direction, we obtain a good view of Guingamp and of the country round. There is a mound, covered with smooth grass, clumps of gorse, and tall fir trees, through which the wind moans on the calmest day; a spot much favoured on summer evenings by the youth of Guingamp. Looking round over the thickly wooded but rather sombre landscape, and on the old grey roofs of the town, one is a little at a loss to account for the rapturous descriptions which nearly all travellers give of. Guingamp. On a fine summer's morning the landscape is seen to perfection; but to tell the truth about it, the scene is not very striking either for beauty or for colour. Guingamp has been described as "a diamond set in emeralds," and we read of its landscape "riant," and so on. "Guingamp m'a pris le cœur," says another traveller; but their interest is in the past, they people it with memories, and with the events of past years.

Our business is with the present aspect of Brittany, and we are bound to record that Guingamp, excepting at the time of the Pardon, is a very ordinary place indeed. The artist and the angler may linger in its valleys, and make it headquarters for many an excursion. If we might suggest one walk to them, we should say—

Go out of the town in a south-easterly direction, following the course of the river Trieux on its right bank for half an hour, and you will come to a suburban village, with a rough wooden cross (like the one sketched on page 89) raised aloft in the centre of the street, and the bright and trim new stone spire of a chapel conspicuous amongst its irregular roof-tops.

Turn round to the right hand, just by the cross, and enter a large farmyard; the women are busy winnowing, not with hands upraised in the wind, as we have seen them at St. Brieuc, but twirling by hand a new patent blue-painted rotatory winnowing-machine with a burring sound, in a cloud of choking dust. They are storing their harvest in a large barn, the remains of an ancient Gothic church, the abbey of Ste. Croix, with its choir window piled up with straw. Immediately in front are the farm buildings, part of a round tower and a corner turret standing, and much of the old woodwork and massive interior fittings is still preserved. The garden reaches to the river, where ancient and historic trout disregard the angler of to-day. The farm and its surroundings are as picturesque as any painter could desire.

The inhabitants of this suburb have a real grievance; they had lived for generations in familiar sight and sound of the cathedral of Guingamp; they saw its spire and towers at evening, standing out sharp and clear against the western sky, and were in feeling living almost in the town itself, when suddenly the engineers of the "Chemin de Fer de l'Ouest" threw up a mountain of earth in their midst, and shut out the town and the sunset light from them, and from their children, for evermore.

CHAPTER IV.

LANLEFF — PAIMPOL — LANNION — PERROS-GUIREC.

TWELVE miles north-east of Guingamp is Lanleff—"the land of tears," celebrated for one of the most curious architectural monuments in Brittany, the circular temple of Lanleff. Leaving Guingamp, we pass through a solitary wooded country, the undulating road soon rising high above the valley of the Trieux. The air is fresh and invigorating, and the views from the summits of the hills extend over a wide range of land. At Gommenech we enter the valley of the Leff that we passed at Châtelaudren. There is no prettier river, or one that should more truly delight an artist's eye, than the Leff in its long, winding journey from the mountains to the sea.

Sheltered by woods, shut in here and there by granite walls, with ruins crowning the heights, between green banks and through sloping fields, it is one of those picturesque rivers which are peculiar to Brittany of which we seldom hear mention, but which many an English angler knows well. The view of Gommenech is to be remembered as we cross the valley on our way to the temple of Lanleff; the temple is in ruins, and partially unroofed, but enough remains of the original nave supported by pillars, and its outer circle of aisles, to give us a perfect idea of the structure, which resembles closely and has, doubtless, the same origin as the round churches in England built by the Crusaders on their return from the Holy Land. The diameter of the church to the walls of the outer aisles is not more than 20 feet; in the inner circle, or nave, the twelve arches are round and Romanesque in style, with rude carvings on the capitals. A chancel was afterwards built into the original structure, so that the unroofed walls of the temple formed, as it were, a vestibule to the parish church, and in this circular open porch, under the shadow of a yew-tree, the congregations used to kneel. But the people now assemble in the new parish church on the hillside, and the temple is kept for show. The "holy well with its blood-stained stone" is pointed out to visitors; the pieces of oolite, that encircle the well, show shining red spots when wetted, to mark the place where, according to tradition, "an avaricious priest received money from a father who sold his child to the Evil One."

We listen to the story gravely, and certainly no sign of doubt, or of levity, passes over the grave face of the Breton woman who tells it; we are in a land of historic monuments and traditions of the past, and the people who live at Lanleff are too wise even to smile at the interest travellers take in these things. The story has been handed down from father to son, from mother to daughter, and is now passed on to tourists who can master a little of the Breton tongue.

Continuing our journey northward, we soon arrive at the summit of a hill overlooking the bay of Paimpol and the thickly wooded country round; we have passed good country-houses on the route, with flower-gardens skirted by hanging woods; and as we approach Paimpol, there are houses scattered in sheltered bays, with fishing and pleasure boats aground; an old church surrounded closely by houses, a little *Place*, a custom-house, a quay, boatmen, and fisher-women; but—where is the water? It has retreated for more than a mile, and the long bay or estuary and the port of Paimpol are a desolate waste of mud. Paimpol is a small but busy fishing village, much frequented in summer by the French for bathing. It is not fashionable, but the inns are comfortable, and the country is full of attractions for the summer visitor. The houses on the *Place* and in the narrow streets are old and weather-worn; some are dark and mysterious-looking, and have that peculiar smuggling aspect with which we soon become familiar on this coast.

In a corner of the quiet churchyard of Paimpol there reposes at full length, in stone, "L'Abbé Jean Vincent Moy," many years *curé* of this place and honorary canon of St. Brieuc; and round about him, placed thickly in rows, the former inhabitants of Paimpol rest under black wooden crosses. The *curé* is carved in dark green stone, from which time has taken the sharpness of the chiselling; but the expression is life-like, representing him in the popular act of blessing. There is a cup of holy water at his feet, supplied by an old woman who kneels before the tomb on the damp ground. It is her pious office to guard the tomb of her pastor, and brush off the leaves which fall thickly from the grove of elms overhead. They move slowly and die leisurely at Paimpol; this old woman's time is not yet, for she "has only eighty years." In four newly made graves there repose Eugénie, Marie, Mathilde, and Hortense, and their respective ages are eighty-two, eighty-four, eighty-eight, and eighty-nine!

At Paimpol in summer every one seems to take life easily, the French visitors driving about, bathing, boating, and living perpetually in the fresh, pure air; the native inhabitants getting up boat-races, and dancing the "gavotte" at night, in streets lighted by paper lanterns in old Breton fashion, as we see sketched at Châteauneuf du Faou. There is unusual brightness on this sombre, storm-washed shore; there is the dazzle of a crimson pennant, and the flashing of a snow-white sail; there are green banks, in contrast to water of the deepest blue, for in these little inlets of the sea the summer sun clothes everything with brightness in a moment. Perhaps we have seen Paimpol *en couleur de rose*, for there has been blue sky overhead nearly every day for a fortnight, and the sun is so hot at midday that the market-women put up their red umbrellas, and the men descend into cool cellars for shelter and refreshment.

There is a favourite walk, of about a mile, to a promontory on the south side of the port, by a pathway skirting fields of corn and buckwheat, which brings us to high ground and a shady plantation

of firs, where we lose sight of Paimpol itself, but obtain the best idea
of the surrounding scenery. We choose this walk a little before
sunset on a day when there is a high tide. At our feet, on the left
hand, is a steep bank with tree-tops *below*, their dark foliage con-
trasting with the blue of the water and the orange stems of weather-
worn firs. Looking far away northward and eastward across the
water, dotted with white sails coming in with the tide, the island
rocks light up brilliantly in the setting sun. The air is so clear
seaward that we can distinguish little houses on the island which
guards the port, and on more distant rocks far out to sea, all glittering
in the sun. Turning southward, to the real bay of Paimpol, which we
cannot see from the town, the opposite banks are in shadow, and the
foliage which reaches to the water's edge takes a rich purple tinge.
The outlines are soft and indistinct, excepting on a tongue of land
in the middle of the bay, where in the midst of a garden of fruit-trees,
and surrounded by ivy-grown walls, we can just trace the Gothic lines
of the abbey of BEAUPORT.

It is a shaded walk of about a mile and a half from Paimpol
to Beauport. The road and the by-paths are shut in by high
banks, so that we come upon it rather suddenly, looking down upon
the ruins, through the bare windows of which we can see the
sea. The Gothic chapel is a complete ruin, but part of the abbey
building is in good preservation, and inhabited. One room is turned
into a school-house, and a great roofless hall, once the refectory,
is used as a threshing-floor. The romantic aspect of the ruins of
Beauport, with its surrounding scenery, has been described in every
book on Brittany, and the view of it by moonlight over the bay
of Paimpol is as famous as that of "fair Melrose." To this ancient
abbey come pilgrims of the nineteenth century to study and wonder
at the art of life shown by the monks of the thirteenth. If ever
there was a spot where nature and art seem combined for man's
special enjoyment, it must have been at Beauport. Here the fruitful
land meets the bountiful sea, and there is no arid line of demarcation ;
the corn waves at the water's edge, and the flowers bloom and shed

their leaves into the water. The soil is rich, and the air is soft, and
in this autumn time the harvest seems everywhere ready to man's
hand—a harvest of fruit and grain on land, a harvest of fish and rich
seaweed spread at every tide upon the shore.

The abbey of Beauport is considered by M. Merrimée to be "the
most perfect example of the monastic architecture of the thirteenth
century"—in fact, the most important and beautiful ruin in Brittany.

> " It lies
> Deep-meadow'd, happy, fair with orchard-lawns
> And bowery hollows, crown'd with summer sea."

As we wander round the gardens and through the avenues of trees
that line the raised walks on the breakwater, or under the shadow of
high brick walls, laden with old fruit-trees, it is easy to realise in our
minds the lives of its former occupants. The picturesqueness of Beauport, especially the view, from the eastern side, of the chapter-house
and other dwellings, should attract artists. This afternoon there is
one large white umbrella planted firmly in the gravel of its deserted
walks, and one canvas spread with a green landscape in which old,
grey, mullioned windows, and the stems of weather-beaten trees, form
prominent features.

From Paimpol to Lannion is twenty miles by the road, crossing
the river Trieux by a lofty suspension bridge at Lézardrieux, and
halting at the ancient cathedral town of Tréguier by the way.

TRÉGUIER, as will be seen on the map, is well situated for exploring
the coast and for visiting a variety of places of interest in the neighbourhood ; and it is a town in which the artist and the antiquary
would desire to stay. The cathedral with its graceful spire, "percée au
jour," and its old market-place, with the streets leading from it, form
pictures more characteristic and interesting than anything we have
seen in Dinan or Guingamp. Tréguier, which was one of the four
original bishoprics of Brittany, abounds in historical associations.
Everywhere we hear of "St. Ives," or "St. Yves" (the lawyers'
patron saint), who lived here in the thirteenth century, and who is

E

buried in the cathedral by the side of Duke John V. From Tréguier to the sea there is a wide estuary, capable of floating, at high tide, vessels of large tonnage; and it was here that the famous expedition against England by "Constable Clisson" in the fourteenth century was to have embarked. The shipbuilding which is carried on at Tréguier and the views on the banks of the estuary are not the least picturesque points to notice. The cathedral is in a variety of styles; it has a

north porch of Norman work, and a square tower, "the tower of Hastings," of the eleventh or twelfth century, and some beautiful cloisters of the fifteenth. It might be worth while to stay at Tréguier if only to examine and sketch the interior of an old Breton farmhouse in the neighbourhood, containing the bed of "St. Ives," and other relics of the patron saint; here too we are within easy reach of the remains of the castle of "La Roche Derrien," with its fine views northward over the sea.

It is near Tréguier that we make the discovery of a watering-place, Perros-Guirec, where we can live in the height of the summer season for five francs a day, and where it is difficult to spend more. The bay of Perros-Guirec is just sufficiently off the track of tourists to make it delightful in summer. There are two small inns on the shore, one at either extremity: but the actual village of Perros-Guirec is situated amongst the trees which crown the northern promontory of the bay; there are a few summer-houses and gardens, an old church, and near it a convent, where in July and August strangers may board for a small sum.

It seems hard to break up the peace of this retreat by printing a description of it, but here, we are bound to record, is a spot where we can spend our summer days with the greatest delight. We can live as we like, dress as we like, bathe in the water at our feet, sit and sketch in the shade of woods, through the branches of which we see the shining sea. The air, so fresh and bracing, sweet with the breath of pines, is more grateful in the hot summer months than at Dinard or Trouville, and the sights and sounds are certainly more healthful and restful.

It is evening as we return from a walk by the sea north of Perros-Guirec; before us is a wide and beautiful bay, extending for nearly half a mile in a noble curve of shore ; it is shut off from the land by sloping hills, and bounded at either extremity by rocks. The tide is nearly out, and the sand is as pure, smooth, and untrodden, as on Robinson Crusoe's island. There are no projecting rocks or stones on this wide plain, nothing to be seen on its surface but our long dark shadows and two little crabs, behind their time, making hard for the retreating water. We cross the bay leisurely, treading lightly on the carpet of sand, and watching the sunset light on the rocks and on the little islands which make this coast such a terror to navigators. They are smiling this evening in that roseate hue which storm-washed red granite rocks put forth on gala days, and their purple reflections in the water are as deep and glowing as from the steep walls of the Lago di Garda under an October sun.

The two crabs soon disappear in the water, but as we cross the bay, two other little spots appear at some distance on the sand. The sight is so unusual here that the thought of Crusoe on his island occurs again, and we approach cautiously. The objects are larger and farther off than at first appeared, in fact nearly a quarter of a mile ; they consist of two neat little bundles of clothing, one of which appears to be a silk dress surmounted by a white straw hat ! There is nothing near them but sand, no sign of human creature; but, presently looking seaward, the mystery is explained by two heads appearing suddenly on the surface of the sea, one with long hair

floating from it.   We beat a retreat and learn afterwards that an
evening walk in "ce pays ici" is often supplemented by an evening
bath.   Thus Monsieur and Madame, strolling together on the sands,
make a diversion without ceremony or "machines," and without the
slightest "mauvaise honte."

A little to the north of Perros-Guirec is the village of Ploumanach,
almost built out into the sea.   It is a place to be visited above all
others on this coast for its wildness, and to see the hardy fishing
population, living amongst a loose mass of rocks, nearly surrounded
by water.   Looking northward, on a clear day, we may see a group
of islands that form, as it were, outworks of granite protecting the land
from the waves that break upon this shore.   One of these islands, the
abode of innumerable wild-fowl, is said, with doubtful authority, to be
the Island of Avalon, or Avilion, where King Arthur was buried.

All round these rocky promontories the inhabitants live more on
the sea than on the land ; they look to the sea for their harvest, and
glean on the shore rather than in the fields.   The children of this
seafaring community, when tired of the earth, take to the water
naturally, and it is not an uncommon thing to see the mother of a
family rush from her cottage, lift up her skirts deftly, and jump into
the sea to the rescue.

The principal town in this neighbourhood is LANNION ; it is a
natural commercial centre for the surrounding districts, collecting and
dispersing the produce of the sea and of the shore, and busy also in
providing and fitting out vessels for the mackerel-fisheries.   It is a
busy town, with a fixed population of about 7000, but apparently with
accommodation, and occupation in the busy seasons of spring and
autumn, for a much larger number.   Lannion dates from the twelfth
century.   It is picturesquely situated on the steep slope of hills above
the river Guier.   The market-place in the centre of the town. from
which steep streets descend to the river, is remarkable for its curious
old houses, but nearly all traces of local costume have vanished.   So,
too, has vanished the antique tapestry representing the story of
Coriolanus, and "a staircase up which a regiment of grenadiers

could march in double columns," which used to be shown at the
Hôtel de l'Europe. In their stead we find plate-glass shop fronts,
good pavements, and little children seated on dirty doorsteps dressed
à la parisienne. On market-days the country people come in wearing
their old costumes, and a few well-to-do farmers and their wives, who

put up at the best inns, are dressed in the old homely fashion of the
Bretons of the Côtes-du-Nord.

Lannion, at the time of writing, may be said to be one of the
outposts of French tourist civilisation in the Côtes-du-Nord. Hither
come in summer-time a few Parisians, and families from the interior,
for the bathing; driving to and from Perros-Guirec and other places

on the coast daily, but seldom actually staying on the seashore. In their train come the latest fashions, both in manners and in dress, and it is here we may notice, especially on Sundays and fêtes, the strange contrasts in costume between the Bretons and "the French," as the natives persist in calling their visitors.

It is on their way down to the Jardin Anglais one Sunday morning that a gay Parisian and his wife walk through the market-place and down one of the old steep streets; behind them come nurse and *bébé*, all "en grande toilette de l'été." The lady wears a white dress, which trails over the cobblestones; the gentleman is in brown holland, with white shoes, white tie, and a new straw hat shaped like a Prussian helmet and decorated with a crimson band; the baby is decorated in as much of the fashion of the day as its size will permit; the nurse, the neatest of the party, wears a spotless white cap and dark short dress. An old dame, seated at her doorstep, taking a bountiful pinch of snuff, emits a harsh sound, more like "Jah!" or "Yah!" than the customary approving "Jolie!" which comes so trippingly on every French tongue. The Breton woman, in her old-fashioned gown, black stockings, and neat stout shoes, who owns the house she lives in, and perhaps half a dozen others, regards the fashionable visitors with anything but pleasure, and resists the advance of fashion into Lannion as an evil almost equal to an inroad of Prussians.

In Lannion the most interesting buildings will be found in the neighbourhood of the Grande Place, where some curious slated "hoods," and projecting roofs, break up the perpendicular lines of the modern buildings; enough remaining even now to account for the frequent descriptions of its picturesqueness. The church of St. Jean, with its high terrace overlooking the valley, is interesting principally from its commanding position above the town. From its terraces and between the stems of its dusty trees there is a pretty sight on Sunday morning when the people crowd to the neighbouring church of Brélévenez.

Looking northwards across a deep ravine—through which a once clear, rapid stream rushes full of soap into the river Guier—we see that in course of time it has worn its way through rocks, washed the slight covering of earth from the roots of trees that grow on its steep sides, that it has been utilised to turn water-wheels, dashing in and out of holes in wooden houses built over its banks. It has "washed" for Lannion for hundreds of years, and every summer's evening down by the bridge, the women, old and young, may be seen on their knees at work on wet boards. On the opposite side of the ravine the houses rise one above the other in a series of steps to the church of Brélévenez with its fine spire cresting the hill; and it is up and down these steps that on Sundays and fête days the people crowd in a dark procession all day. The ascent is steep indeed, and the young have to help the old to make the pilgrimage.

If we follow the crowd across the ravine and up this narrow way, we find that it has been selected by suffering and poverty-stricken humanity as a public mart. The path is so narrow and steep that there is no escape from the beggars that line the way. In the church-yard at the top it is a pretty sight to see the country people meeting and chatting together under the trees, standing in groups waiting for the service. They are evidently accustomed to the beggars; but it seems hard upon Marie and Mathilde, coming on a summer's morning through the fields to church, to have to run the gauntlet of so much misery and disease, to have hideous deformities thrust upon their sight, and curses hurled at them if they do not give. A stranger is of course fair game—he is Dives, and Lazarus is waiting for him at the gate; but all are importuned alike, and every hideous artifice is used to extract alms under the protection of the church. The women and children push their way bravely, slipping over the stone stiles modestly one by one, their neat short skirts being suited to the work. The air is fresh and sweet, blowing through the churchyard; but inside the church the crowd is great, and the heat almost insufferable. The beggars do not go in, at least not many of them, but they lie in wait and line the descent of this ladder of life, sunning themselves in corners until the pilgrims pass down.

Before leaving Lannion, a word should be said about the inn

accommodation, because it is exceptionally good. They may be small matters to record in print, but it will be useful to travellers to know that in Lannion they will find at the principal inn the comforts of civilisation, including an excellent cup of tea. After a few days' stay at the Hôtel de l'Europe the illusion will be dispelled that in travelling in Brittany, away from railways, it is necessary to "rough it," as the saying is. In all the principal towns on our route the hotels will be found as good as in Normandy and other parts of western France; and throughout Brittany we get abundance of good meat, bread, butter, milk, and wine. At the Hôtel de l'Europe at Lannion, English families come to stay, it being quieter and less crowded than Dinan, as well as a convenient centre for visiting some of the most interesting spots in Brittany; interesting to English people especially for their historical and romantic associations.

Everyone makes a short stay at Lannion, in order to visit the thirteenth-century castle of Tonquédec, in a lovely valley about eight miles south of the town. It is easy to reach it by taking one of the diligences on the road to Guingamp to a point about five miles from Lannion, or by taking a carriage direct. At the time of writing, this castle is one of the best preserved specimens of military architecture in all France, and it is to our mind one of the beauty spots in Brittany. Time has covered its towers and walls with thick and luxuriant foliage, graceful in line, and altogether picturesque from its untrimmed aspect; in autumn time it is as rich in colour as a pheasant's wing, and the lines of the landscape which surround it are as varied as the waves of the sea.

The castle of Tonquédec was one of the ancient strongholds of Brittany; the present structure is in great part the restoration of Henry IV., and the ruin the work of Cardinal Richelieu; time and ivy having done the rest. It is rare to find, as at Tonquédec, so "complete a ruin," if we may use the word, showing the plan and structure of its different courts, its fortifications, and surrounding dwellings, as used in the thirteenth century. We must not dwell upon architectural details, but we may mention the views that are to be obtained from its windows and towers, the adjoining park and avenues of old trees, and the lake with its ancient carp asleep under the banks, who—according to the women in charge of the castle—"have lived so long that their tails are worn out"!

At Lannion and Tonquédec we are on the border-land which divides the departments of the Côtes-du-Nord and Finistère. The little river Douron, which takes its source in the Monts d'Arrée, and falls into a bay between Plestin and Lanmeur, marks the boundary of the departments and also of the ancient bishoprics of Tréguier and St. Pol de Léon. There is a natural division between the two departments in the general aspect of the country and demeanour of the people. From the hanging gardens of Beauport and the sleepy orchards and cornfields which surround Lannion and Tonquédec we shall shortly pass to a wilder and sterner part of the coast, dominated by the cathedral spires of St. Pol and Le Folgoet.

CHAPTER V.

THUS far we have spoken of the northern coast, where the busy inhabitants of the Côtes-du-Nord come most in contact with French traders, and travellers of different nations. Let us now turn towards the mountains, where the country is less fertile, the people are more isolated, and there is more character and local costume to be seen.

If we leave the Western Railway at Guingamp or Belle-Isle-en-Terre, we may follow the course of the streams which take their rise in the Monts d'Arrée, and, passing through Callac, reach Carhaix the same evening. We cross the purple mountains where the solitary shepherd in goat's-skin coat (sketched on page 68) tends his flocks on poor pastures, and where the, almost equally solitary, Englishman is busy with a fly-rod. At Callac, where comfortable quarters are to be obtained, many Englishmen stay for the fishing and shooting seasons; the streams are well stocked with fish, and there is little difficulty in getting permission for fishing.

The game laws are very strict in France, as is well known; the opening and closing of the shooting season varies every year, the prefect deciding the day in September when shooting may begin. The *chasse courant*, which includes hunting the wolf and the wild-boar, commences about a month later. The seasons close at the end of January, and whenever snow is on the ground. Altogether there is more attraction for the angler than for the sportsman in Brittany, and there is no better centre for the angler than Callac.

The aspect of the people and their dwellings in this neighbourhood is more simple and primitive than we have yet seen; and the features of the peasants are more strongly marked with the privations of generations. It is the same dull round of life, labour, and hardship, with a few gleams of sunshine in summer; and a Pardon and a blessing from the priest at the annual fête. There is the same story everywhere. "We move slowly; we do as our fathers did, and live contentedly as they lived."

How did they live sixty years ago? An Englishman who spent some time in Brittany in 1818 says of the peasants:—"They are rude, uncivilised, simple, and dirty in their habits; they live literally like pigs, lying upon the ground and eating chestnuts boiled in milk as their principal food. Their houses are generally built of mud, without order or convenience, and it is a common thing in Brittany for men, women, children, and animals to sleep together in the same apartment, upon no resting-place but the earth covered with straw."[*] This was written sixty years ago, but the mud houses are before us, and the description holds good to-day. Forty years later a writer in an English newspaper is sent to report upon the state of the agricultural labourer in Brittany; what does he find? "The Breton peasant," he says,[†] "is still isolated from the towns by his language. He has kept himself apart, and mistrusts the outer world. His fare is black bread, made of buckwheat, or rye, oats or barley, boiled with milk. If he have a change in his diet, it is in the shape of potatoes. His life is an unbroken monotony. He never changes his manners, his habits, or his dress. He is a stranger in the large towns, where even his language is not understood, save by a few people who deal with him. He is as patient and quiet as a beast of burden; his daily hard labour seems to subdue even his affections, it leaves

---

[*] Stothard's *Brittany*, 1820.   [†] Blanchard Jerrold's Letters to the *Morning Post*, 1853-60.

him no time for grief, no hours for the indulgence of remorse, no
moment for despair."

Twenty years later, what do we find? Excepting in a few districts,
such as that near Lannion, where there is a considerable advance in
agriculture, and where the peasant's position is better, we find the same
figure wearing the same coat, standing just where he did ; his life the

same weary round of labour by day, and rest in
an old mud hovel at sundown.   The problem of
a life of labour and monotony is yet unsolved ; he
is just where he was in 1850, and where his father
was in 1820.   The great Chemin de Fer de
l'Ouest, that was to do so much for the owners
of the land and the tillers of the fruitful soil of
Brittany, which has been driven through the heart
of the country, with its enormous viaducts and
its trains of cattle trucks ; which has thrown up
embankments of earth that shut him off from

the rest of the world, appear to have done little good.   A train
rushes past his patch of land several times a day, and perhaps his
priest is in it, on his way to Paris or Rennes ; it no longer startles
his children or his pigs, for it has passed now for years ; but "traffic,"
or what is generally understood by the term, scarcely exists, and
passengers, excepting in summer, are few and far between.

A step higher than the peasant, and we find the farm people,
all working on in the old grooves, and, excepting in the matter
of sending their children by train to be educated (which to a
certain extent is compulsory), and in the gradual use of modern
agricultural implements, showing little signs of change.   Nearly all
the farms are worked on a small scale, and with the least employ-
ment of capital.   "Thrift, thrift !" is the watchword with them all ;
early and late they labour, man, woman, and child, and year by year
gain a little on the past ; a piece more land, a few hundred francs
put by ; but they live on in the same humble, penurious way, with
little care or trouble about the outer world, and knowing little of its

movements. Their very charities are an investment by the teaching
of their own church: a sou is given to a beggar without grudging, for
shall it not be repaid? Thus on the one side we may contemplate
a life of work and thrift, which is admirable, and a conservatism
which keeps the soil in the hands of the labourer; but on the other,
the view is of a race behindhand in civilisation, wanting in knowledge and in sympathy with the rest of mankind.

We descend the hills from Callac, following the course of the river
Aven to CARHAIX, the ancient capital of a province and the centre of
a large agricultural district, owing its present importance to its cattle
fairs. At ordinary times life is peaceful enough at Carhaix; in the
principal square is the Hôtel de la Tour d'Auvergne, where visitors
can live as comfortably as in any country town in France, and where
the days resemble one another very closely. Every afternoon the
people sit and sun themselves in the principal square, as in the

sketch below, and pigs lie down undisturbed in the middle of the
street; every evening the inhabitants walk under the trees on the
dingy *Place*, with its avenues of limes, where there is a fine view
over the country, and where is Marochetti's bronze statue of La Tour
d'Auvergne, " le premier grenadier de France."

Between two and three o'clock in the afternoon there is the only
communication with the outer world, when, with much cracking of
whips and rattling over stones, a crazy vehicle called "the courier,"
with its lame and battered horse, covered with dust and foam, comes

lumbering in. It brings a packet of newspapers, chiefly local; for
Carhaix cares little for the doings of the world beyond that of which
it is the centre. But we must now speak of the fair.

Six roads converge upon Carhaix, and upon these roads, and
across the open land, on a summer's morning, comes a stream of horses,
cattle, pigs, and people. It is the day of the cattle fair, a day for
meeting and marketing for all the country round; a day of rejoicing,
bargaining, and of cruelty to animals scarcely to be paralleled elsewhere;
the day and the place to see the Breton farmers and cattle-dealers,
to study the costumes and the ways of the peasants from some of
the most primitive districts of Brittany.

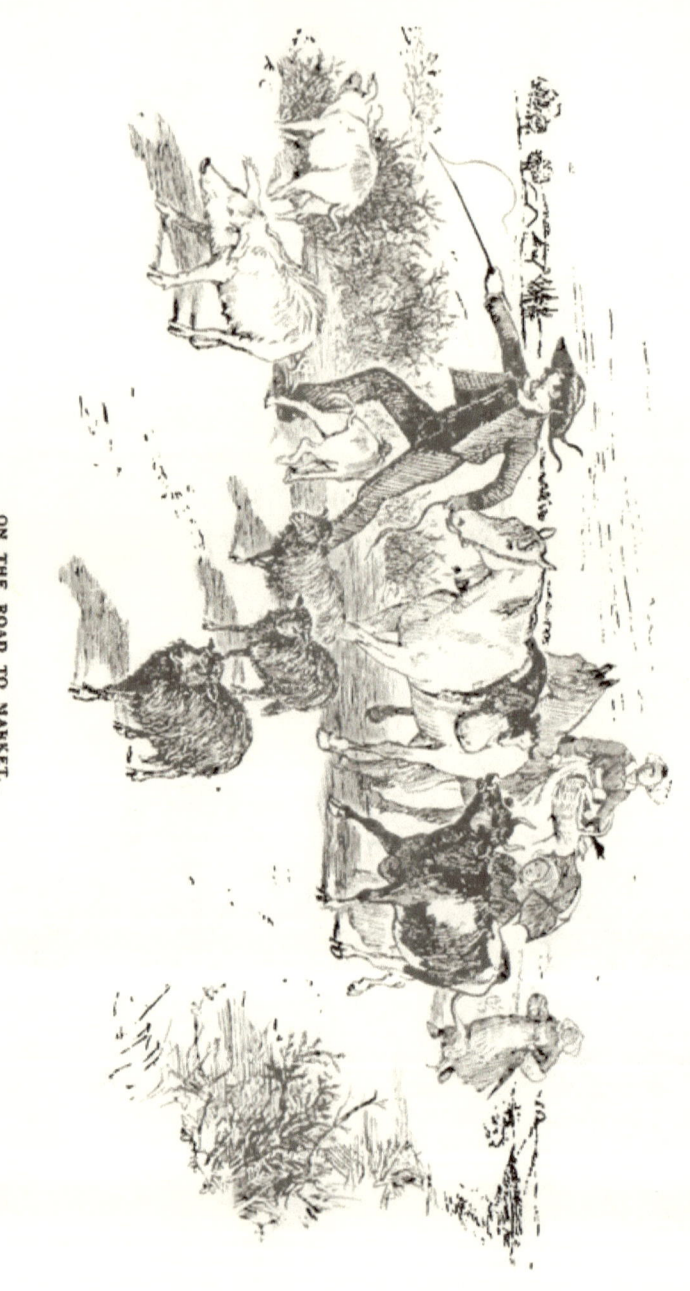

ON THE ROAD TO MARKET.

It is only four o'clock in the morning, but the sounds of shouting (in strong Breton tones, which seem to Englishmen a perpetual echo from the Welsh hills), the lowing of cattle, the shrieking of pigs, and the heavy thud of sabots resound upon the roads. On the rising ground just outside Carhaix, on the western road, we can see them through an avenue of trees coming across the country in narrow defile, like the commissariat train of an army on the march ; the men leading cattle, the women on horseback and on foot, laden with provisions ; and others in holiday attire, arriving in country carts.

The sun shines full on the wrinkled faces of the men, and on the white caps of the women, and lights up the group with unwonted brilliancy ; even the sober costumes of the people with their blue and brown stuffs, and the black, and white and fawn-coloured, cattle which they lead, would, if recorded faithfully by a painter, stand out in high accents of colour against the low-toned land ; a rustic picture so fitful and vanishing that only the rapid artist, who has presented Brittany to us in these pages (as it has never been pictured before), could depict. It is the sunny side of Brittany in all its quaintness, the pastoral aspect of life which those who dwell in cities seldom see. There is nothing to mar the beauty of the morning, for the noise of the market is as yet a distant sound, mingled with the bells of Carhaix for early mass; there is nothing to suggest a change but the gathering of the clouds towards the west, and the stout umbrellas and cloaks carried by the women.

Let us follow them, later in the day, to a large square where the fair is held, and where there are wonderful sights and sounds; under

the trees a crowd of men and women, in the dust and heat, horses, cattle, and pigs, in perpetual movement, with much drinking and shouting at the booths which line one side of the enclosure. There are a great many horses for sale, which do not find buyers, although the government agents are here from the neighbouring *haras* at Callac, and horse-dealers have come from all parts. The cattle market is overstocked, and the little black and white cattle, a cross between Alderneys and Bretons, go for very small sums to reluctant purchasers. The pig market is more active, as every Breton peasant

CATTLE FAIR AT CARHAIX.

likes to possess a pig, and the noises proceeding from this part of the square are deafening. The gentleman farmer in blue blouse to keep off the dust is the portrait of a prominent figure moving amongst the crowd.

The meetings of the country people, and the groups sitting under the trees to rest, are as suggestive pictures as we have seen, and the costumes are full of variety and interest; the whole forms a scene

of which the full-page sketch gives an accurate idea. These markets are held several times a year, and for a few hours disturb the quiet of the sleepy town of Carhaix.

We could well stay at Carhaix, for the scenery is varied and interesting, and there is much to observe in the farmhouses in the neighbourhood; old furniture, old carved bedsteads, cabinets, and clocks; old brasswork, old lace and embroideries.

Pictures come to us at every turn, pictures of domestic happiness and content, only to be seen in byways far removed from cities and

F

their troubles ; family groups, in which our presence seems sometimes
an intrusion. Brittany, like Spain, is a country that should be travelled
through cautiously ; the inhabitants live out of doors in summer-time,
and perform various domestic operations in the roads, regardless of traffic.

Turn a corner suddenly and you may come upon a scene of family
discord, or affection, where you are of necessity *de trop ;* take a walk in
the evening in the outskirts of a town, and the mute aspect of the
people, one and all, is that the road belongs to them, that the dirt
and the dunghills of the poorest are heirlooms which no invading
sanitary inspectory shall reform.

In the farmhouses in the neighbourhood we shall often find but one living and sleeping room—kitchen, sitting-room, bedroom, all in one; the bedstead of carved oak, the cupboards and chests with brass handles and bosses, the copper cooking utensils bright and shining, the floor at the same time being of bare earth. There is often a dungheap outside, and a shed for cows opening into the living room, which is common alike to pigs, fowls, and children. We see the women coming out of their dark, unhealthy dwellings on fête-days, looking bright and clean, with old lace in their caps, embroidered shawls, and the neatest of shoes. We see them thrashing corn and scattering the grain wastefully on the ground, and farming on a small scale in primitive fashion. But the Bretons who live thus are nearly all prosperous and thrifty in their own way; they own most of the land

WAITING FOR DINNER, HUELGOET.

they farm, paying rent, for a portion perhaps, at the rate of twenty or twenty-five francs an acre, but adding to the extent of their ownership year by year. Nearly everyone we meet at Carhaix is engaged in agriculture, and the majority are well-to-do. The land yields well, and there is the Canal de Brest passing through the town to take the produce to the coast.

Turning northwards towards Morlaix, we pass through somewhat dreary scenery, until we come to a gorge near Huelgoet, which, with its rocks and rushing streams, will remind us of Switzerland;

here are some ancient lead and silver mines, which were a source of considerable wealth in the fifteenth century.

There is a silent and deserted air about the streets of Huelgoet, seldom disturbed by the sound of wheels ; at the inn where we rest our dinner is cooked in the *salle à manger* at the open fireplace, and from the manner of the people it is evident strangers are rare, even in summer. We are asked by the taciturn landlord to take up our abode here "for the sake of the fishing," and a book is shown containing the names of visitors who have staid at the inn.

The road between Huelgoet and Morlaix, passing over a spur of the Monts d'Arrée, is again wild and desolate ; we see flocks scattered over barren pastures, and men and women at work on open ground far away from habitations. It is a suggestive part of Brittany for the landscape painter, a dark lonely land of rugged outline, full of poetry and mystery.

CHAPTER VI.

MORLAIX — ST. POL — LESNEVEN — LE FOLGOET.

FROM the quiet of Carhaix and the solemn landscape which surrounds Huelgoet to the bustle of Morlaix, only sixteen miles to the north, seems a rapid transition. If we arrive at Morlaix by railway, we cross a lofty viaduct over a deep ravine, and, far below, see clusters of grey roofs, white houses, rocks and trees, church towers, and factory chimneys. Descending to the town, we find ourselves in the centre of more commercial activity than we have seen since leaving St. Malo. Morlaix is a prosperous town, containing about 15,000 inhabitants, busily engaged in trade. It is built at the confluence of two streams, the Jarlot and the Queffleut, which meet in the centre of the city, and (arched over for some distance in their course) wind down the valley to the sea, six miles away. On either side of this canal-like stream are quays, and rows of houses, old and new, strangely intermixed.

The commercial traveller, the shipper of native products, and the importer of foreign goods is ever busy at Morlaix. But its aspect is still essentially old ; its outward characteristics are primitive : weather-worn gables with carved beams, steep streets and rough pavements with open gutters, and, in the centre of the city, a dingy river, with washerwomen on its banks   The sketch gives an exact idea of the scene as enacted every day in the principal street; but the old architecture of Morlaix is best indicated on page 72. A few demolitions take place every year, but, visiting Morlaix for the

third time in 1878, we find the most interesting buildings standing and leaning against each other as of old. Tradition is strong in this city, and many new shops preserve over their doors their old signs, the ancient insignia of the trades of the merchants of Morlaix. Some are grotesque figures carved in wood, painted and gilt; there is one little figure, for instance, at the corner of the Rue Notre Dame, "Au Sonneur Breton," in cocked hat and curled wig, which carries us back in imagination several centuries.

In the "Rue des Nobles," where the high-pitched roofs and overhanging eaves nearly meet across the street, we may see the actual dwellings of the nobles of Brittany in the fifteenth century, whilst above on the steep hillsides, and all around, are the modern, meaner, and more healthy dwellings of the traders of the nineteenth.

The approach to Morlaix by water in the old days, when at the last turn of the river the pointed gables and towers came into view, must have been very picturesque. Its aspect in 1505, when the nobles received the Queen-Duchess Anne on her pilgrimage through Brittany, and later—when Mary Queen of Scots landed here on her way to Paris to espouse the Dauphin in 1548—we may picture to ourselves, with some regret, as we walk down the new wide Rue de Brest, and see above us the great railway viaduct. It is a strange medley of grey roofs, trees, rocks, towers, factory chimneys, quays lined with stores, precipitous streets, tottering dwellings, and defaced churches (one turned into a granary), arched over by the modern railway viaduct, from the view of which there is no escape, but which, from its very height and solidity, has a certain grandeur of effect. But the old is quite overwhelmed by the new, and even the steep hillsides seem dwarfed by the giant proportions of the viaduct. There is not only more movement, but there is more colour in Morlaix, than we are accustomed to in Brittany; down on the quay, for instance, there are red sashes, and clothing of bright Oriental hues, drying in the wind; and there is a certain Eastern air about the open shops in the old quarters which tells of distant commerce. But the present prosperity of Morlaix is in its tobacco manufactories, in its trade in butter, grain, fruit, &c., and in its position as the natural place of export for the products of a fruitful part of Brittany.

It is well to stay at Morlaix to make sketches of some of the lofty interiors with their carved staircases, some of which are quite unique; and it is well to see it on Sundays, for nowhere shall we see pleasanter faces or a happier and brighter-looking population. On market mornings the country people crowd the *Place*, and, in the morning and in the evening, five or six hundred factory hands, men and women, pass up and down the

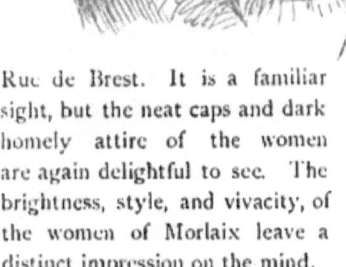

Rue de Brest. It is a familiar sight, but the neat caps and dark homely attire of the women are again delightful to see. The brightness, style, and vivacity, of the women of Morlaix leave a distinct impression on the mind.

In the neighbourhood, in the direction of Brest, are two of the most famous calvaries and churches of the Renaissance, St. Thégonnec and Guimiliau. It is half an hour's journey by train to the little deserted station of St. Thégonnec, on the railway to Brest, and a mile to the north is the village. There is no one at the station but the station-master, and no communication with the village of St. Thégonnec excepting by a covered cart, which meets the morning train. The fine church, which stands in the midst of a straggling village of dilapidated houses, pigsties, and dirt, is rich in sculpture and gilding in the style of the Renaissance ; on the high-altar, on the pulpit, and in the side chapels are elaborate carvings, much overdone with gilding and restoration, but grand in general effect. In the churchyard all is grey, sad-looking, and dilapidated ; the ancient calvary, erected in 1610 in dark Kersanton stone, is injured and time-stained ; the quaint figures, elaborately carved, representing passages in the history of Christ (dressed in ruffs and gowns of the sixteenth century), are roughly propped up and stuck together, for the benefit of pilgrims who come to the shrine.

The calvary of St. Thégonnec, like most others in Brittany, depicts scenes in the life and Passion of Christ. In the centre is a group of three crosses, representing the scene of the Crucifixion, with figures of the centurion and soldiers, angels, and the Virgin and St. John, and on either side are the two thieves. Below, round the base of the structure, are figures in Breton costume, representing the judgment of Pilate, Christ bearing the cross, the Entombment, and the Resurrection. Some of the figures are remarkable for animation, and, in spite of the state of the monument, appeal more powerfully to the imagination than a group of coloured life-size figures representing the Entombment which is shewn to visitors in the crypt.*

The church and calvary of Guimiliau is in a quiet village a few miles to the south-west, a short drive from St. Thégonnec, crossing the railway. The church dates from the Renaissance, and is rich in carving and decoration ; the interior is loaded with ornament, the eastern end being a mass of crude colours and florid decoration. In the south porch is some elaborate carving, and in the organ loft are some bas-reliefs on the oak panels. There is a baptistry of carved oak, consisting of a canopy with allegorical figures, supported on eight spiral pillars, around which are twisted vine leaves, fruit, flowers, and birds. The pulpit, dated 1677, is also a remarkable work of art. But in the churchyard, time-stained and crumbling to

---

* For a sketch of one of the calvaries, see page 91.

decay as usual, is the great object of our visit, a solid stone structure
raised upon arches, upon which is a crowd of little carved figures in
the costume of the sixteenth century, representing the various scenes
of the Passion. There are saints in the niches at the corners, and
high above is a crucifix, with the figures of Mary and St. John on
either side. This monument dates from 1580, but many of the
figures have been restored at a later date.

Altogether the calvaries of St. Thégonnec and Guimiliau, whether
regarded from a picturesque or antiquarian point of view, are the
most interesting monuments we have yet seen ; interesting in their
very loneliness, the object of so much thought and labour in the middle
ages, left thus neglected and in ruin. The calvaries of Brittany seem
little cared for, excepting as curiosities ; but once a year, at Easter
time, there are religious ceremonies connected with them, when special
services are performed, and the various scenes depicted on the
monuments are explained to the people. Then is the time to visit
St. Thégonnec and Guimiliau, when the people are seen gathered round
the sculptured crosses, in the same costumes and in the same attitude
of faith as their forefathers.

From the time we left St. Thégonnec station until our return in
the evening, after visiting these two calvaries, we have seen few
people in the fields or on the roads. The busy city of Morlaix
absorbs all available hands, and leaves the country towns almost
deserted. When the railway was advanced at an enormous cost
through a difficult country to the port of Brest, it was thought,
naturally enough, that it would open up traffic *en route;* but here at
St. Thégonnec no one comes. "I live," says the station-master, "in a
vast solitude, the monotony of which is only broken by the passing
of five or six trains a day ; scarcely any one comes near me ; a
stray tourist or two in the summer, and an occasional visit from a
wolf in winter, one of which has killed my favourite dog." This
station-master, whose daughter was being educated at Morlaix, kept
a brood of turkeys for distraction ; but it was "a lonely life," as he
said, a solitude the more keenly felt because he was connected by a

telegraph wire with the headquarters of the administration of the Chemin de Fer de l'Ouest. "It was solitude without peace, for at any moment, day or night, the bell might ring." It is difficult to realise that this is on the main line of railway between Paris and Brest!

There is no stranger or more suggestive contrast for the traveller in Brittany than to leave Morlaix on a summer's morning and drive twelve miles in a north-westerly direction to St. Pol de Léon. It takes only three hours, but in that short journey we pass, as it were, from life to death, from the commercial activity of to-day to a stillness which belongs to the past. The passage is from wharves and warehouses, from crowded factories and the shrieking of steam, to open country, hill and dale, to the sea. In Morlaix the monuments are to commerce, in St. Pol de Léon to the church; in Morlaix there is activity and a certain amount of civilisation, in St. Pol de Léon, by contrast, there is stillness, poverty, and degradation. Our last view of Morlaix is of a stupendous railway viaduct, of comfortable villas and trim gardens; our first view of St. Pol de Léon across the open land is of three noble church spires standing out sharply against the sky. Ancient stone crosses and images of saints in glass cases are passed as usual on the roadside, before we approach Léon, "the Holy City," which five centuries ago, when Morlaix was unknown, was an important bishopric and the centre of great ecclesiastical wealth. To-day its aspect is poor and dreary, even in sunshine; grey and cold in colour, and generally dirty.

But the cathedral with its spires and the tower of the church of Notre Dame de Creizker (nearly 400 feet high) are the absorbing points of interest, the reason of our journey to St. Pol.

The inhabitants, numbering about 7000, are principally agricultural, or are employed at the port; fishermen and knitting women, reserved and dignified in manner, living rough homely lives, disdaining many of the modern ways of Morlaix, but having a keen eye to commerce, which they carry on actively with far-away places, including Norway and Greenland.

As we saunter up the rough, ill-paved streets of the cathedral

square, the men come out of the cafés and *débits de tabac*, and
give us a rough but not unkindly greeting, as in the sketch. The
principal occupation of our three friends is to cultivate potatoes,

cabbages, onions, asparagus, and other vegetables for foreign markets ;
for this part of Brittany forms one vast market-garden, whence the
cities of Western Europe are supplied. The inhabitants who live in the
cathedral square have grown up in perpetual wonderment (expressed
in their faces) at the summer procession of pilgrims to St. Pol de

Léon ; pilgrims in strange costumes, who dispense sous to their children, inquire for the keys of the tower of the Creizker, and then mount several hundred feet above them in the wind.

The cathedral dedicated to St. Pol is a fine example of early Gothic architecture, noble in proportions, rich in carving and sombre in colour, the dark green Kersanton stone giving a fine effect to the interior, in which some white-robed nuns are generally to be seen

on their knees. The nave is thirteenth-century work, there is some florid carving on the south porch, and a fine rose window; above are two towers, with lofty lancet windows, and spires which remind us of churches in Normandy.

But the spire of Notre Dame de Creizker—literally, " Our Lady of the Middle Town "—which is higher than the cathedral towers, is the most interesting object in St. Pol ; the central point round which the lives of the Léonnais radiate, a landmark seen far and wide by land and sea. This spire, built in the fourteenth century, in the reign

of John IV., Duke of Brittany, is supposed to be the work of an
English architect. The tower is of granite, richly ornamented with
a projecting cornice, and its spire is pierced through to the sky.
The beauty and magnificence of the churches of St. Pol de Léon are
out of all proportion to the present importance—or unimportance—of
the place. The inhabitants have little sympathy with the art of the
sixteenth century, or with the Druidical remains they find in their
fields, but they welcome travellers gladly in the nineteenth.

It is a wide plain round about St. Pol, from which the Gothic
spires seem to reach to heaven, and where a human figure, standing
in a field, points upwards with strange emphasis against the sky;
a district peopled by classic-looking market gardeners, whose children
walk in groves of cabbages five feet high, and play at hide and seek
in their shadows.

Three miles north of St. Pol is the little seaport of Roscoff,
historically interesting as the landing-
place of the child princess Mary Queen
of Scots, who passed through Roscoff
on her way to Nantes in 1548. There
are the ruins of a chapel founded by
her, still standing on the seashore; in
the church, with its open belfry tower,
are some curious alabaster reliefs; and in
the neighbourhood, in a convent garden,
is a gigantic fig-tree, said to be two
centuries old. Roscoff is now used as
a bathing-place, and there is a constant
passing to and fro in summer between
this port and a little island three miles
farther north, the Île de Batz, where
a hardy population of fishermen and

GURGOYLE AT ROSCOFF.

women ply their dangerous trade, with hardly any communication
with the shore in winter. It is almost worth while to cross to the Île
de Batz to see the "Druidesses," as the women of the island

are called, assembling on Sundays in their island church; and it might be worth while for a painter to make a longer stay in this neighbourhood, to make studies (if only for colour) of some of the curious figures to be seen in such out-of-the-way corners as Roscoff. Here is one of an old man with long hair and semi-nautical aspect, who sits in the evening on a stone seat in front of the cottage which he owns, facing the sea ; a poor man to outward

appearance, but an owner of the soil ; his face is screwed and weather-worn, his clothes are patched in various shades of brown ; his blouse is of a dark and greasy tinge ; his working life has been spent in the fields or down at the port, but his final cause is undoubtedly to smoke ; he has coloured by degrees, like a good old pipe, and his sabots have caught the true meerschaum tinge; he has smouldered at Roscoff for many years, and seems ready for burning, stacked against the wall like the fagots collected for winter fires. There is no difficulty in making a sketch, for this rich-toned "owner of the soil" of Finistère has a perfect contempt for strangers, and is as immovable as the gurgoyle sketched on the preceding page.

Let us now turn westward in the direction of Lesneven and 'Le Folgoet, to see one of the finest churches in Finistère. There are two roads to Lesneven, of which we would recommend the traveller to take the one to the north, near the sea. The country is for the most part dreary in aspect, but there are some curious wayside crosses on the route. There are a few fields of buckwheat, corn, and rye, banked up by high hedges, and skirted by pollard trees. It is

one of those drives which should be taken leisurely by the antiquary
or the archæologist; a route where there is little to remind us of
the present, and much to bring before us the habits of the past.
Every monument we pass on the road, every hovel at the roadside,
and nearly every peasant in the fields, is of the pattern of a past age.

As we skirt these quiet shores of northern Finistère, we may listen
for a moment to a story just five hundred years old, a story that
every Breton peasant that we pass on the road knows by heart: how

a poor idiot named Salaun, who lived in the neighbourhood of Lesneven for forty years, and begged for his bread in the name of the
Virgin, uttering only the words, "Ave Maria," was found dead by a
fountain and buried on the spot; how a white lily grew upon his
grave, with the words, "Ave Maria," inscribed upon the leaves; and
how John of Blois, then fighting for the dukedom of Brittany, hearing
of the "miracle," vowed that, if successful in battle, he would erect a
church to Notre Dame de Folgoet, *i.e.* "Fool of the Wood."

The church was completed by his son, John V., about 1420. It
was built like most of the churches and monuments of Finistère, of
the dark Kersanton stone found near St. Pol de Léon, and at the

IN THE CHURCH OF LE FOLGOET.

village of Kersanton, near Brest. The church consists of a lofty
nave and aisles under one roof, with a long projecting transept on
the south side. The great beauty of the church is in its carving,
that on the south porch being perhaps the finest. The great west
door, now falling into ruin, is elaborately ornamented with wreaths of
the vine and other devices, and above it is a bas-relief representing
the Nativity and the Adoration of the Shepherds. In the beautiful
south porch, which is supposed to have been added by the Queen-
Duchess Anne, are the arms of Brittany and figures of the twelve
apostles in niches, and round its roof are traces of a richly carved
parapet. In the interior there are five altars, with carved figures of
angels, birds, and flowers; and on the rood-loft, between the choir
and nave, supported upon elaborately carved pillars, is some open
tracery cut in stone, in good preservation. There is a fine rose
window, as at St. Pol de Léon.

The spring, or Fool's Well, is under the high-altar, and the water
flows into a basin *outside* the church. It is here that the sick and
needy come and kneel before a statue of Our Lady set in a Gothic
niche, and bathe their limbs in the water of the miraculous well; a
retired spot, where, at all hours of the day, peasants are to be found
on their knees in prayer.

We have given but slight descriptions of the churches of St. Pol
de Léon and Le Folgoet, but enough to indicate that here at least
the traveller will be rewarded for going out of the beaten track, and
that in Brittany, owing to the wonderful durability of the Kersanton
stone, we can still see the handwork and judge of the skill of the
sculptors of the fourteenth century.

The church of Le Folgoet stands, as guide-books tell us, on "a
silent spot, unvisited save on certain festivals, and removed a mile
and a half from any town." We find it the centre of a tumult
impossible to describe. There is a large horse-fair being held, which
has collected a crowd almost equal to that at Carhaix; but here
there is more variety in the costume of the men, the red Phrygian
caps and sashes lighting up the crowd with unusual colour. It is a

scene strangely in contrast with the quiet of the cathedral, where under its cool arcades men are kneeling, whip in hand; they have come to pray for a special blessing from St. Cornely, the patron saint of cattle.

The men, in light canvas trousers and blue jerseys, standing on the left in the picture of the fair, are horse dealers and agents for the government, who attend every cattle fair and market throughout the country. The men on the right, watching a horse being trotted out, are thoroughly characteristic figures, portraits of well-to-do Breton farmers and dealers.

The boy on the horse is a good example of the Breton *gamin*, or hanger-on at fairs, who trots out the horses with untiring energy, and with a freedom and grace of limb delightful to behold.

CHAPTER VII.

BREST — PLOUGASTEL — CHÂTEAUNEUF DU FAOU.

A T Landerneau we are once more on the high-road to Brest. We have left for a time the dreary wind-blown promontories of the coast, and find shelter in a pleasant valley, surrounded by trees and gardens, and watered by a river which opens out westward into the bay of Brest.

The railway from Landerneau to Brest is carried for the most part at a high level, and from the windows on the *left hand* we obtain beautiful views of the scenery of the bay. Below we can see the stores of timber for naval use, and are otherwise reminded of our approach to a sea-port by the company which collect at the small stations *en route*. In the crowded carriage are old weather-beaten fishermen and countrywomen with market baskets, and, in one corner, two boys with fair fresh faces, set in wide straw hats, bearing upon them the inscriptions of *l'ulcan* and *Vengeance.*

Brest is a naval station of such importance that even travellers in search of the picturesque should not pass it by without a short visit ; the arsenal, docks, and harbour are on a scale of completeness second only to Cherbourg ; moreover, Brest is the most convenient point from which to visit other parts of the coast of Finistère, especially the fishing village of Le Conquet, the abbey of St. Mathieu on the extreme western point of Brittany, and the island of Ouessant. Brest

G 2

is situated on an elevated position on the north side of one of the finest natural harbours in the world, commanding good views from its ramparts and promenades. The population is about 70,000, exclusive of soldiers and sailors; a busy cosmopolitan maritime city, in which there is little of the Breton character to be studied.

In order to realise the beauty of the inland bay of Brest, we must look down again from our imaginary *ballon captif*, and see its blue waters, green banks and woods coming down to the water's edge; the

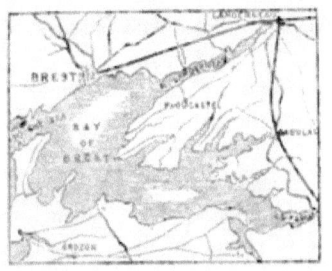

country dotted with white villas and little wooden châlets belonging to the wealthy traders of Brest, and here and there the sombre avenues of a château with grey, high-pitched roofs and pointed turrets peeping through the trees.

Across this inland sea, traversed by little steamers and dotted with white sails—raised high upon the heath-clad hills which form the western spur of the Monts d'Arrée—is the little town of Plougastel.

It is too late to cross the bay on the occasion of our visit to Plougastel, and so we take the last train to Kerhuon station, where there is a ferry. A vessel has just been paid off at Brest, and in the railway carriage are several sailors on their way home. One of them gets out with us at Kerhuon, and we go down together to the river. By some mischance the ferry-boat is missing, and all is darkness at the little boathouse. The young sailor, ready at expedients, puts down his pack, collects some furze, and lights a fire as a signal. We sit and wait and shout at intervals, burning the fuel until just about midnight, when we hear the plash of oars, and a dark object glides past; it is a fishing-boat with one mast, with three men in the stern, and two women rowing. After a little parleying they agree to take us across for thirty centimes each, and the women turn the boat round, running it heavily against the stones of the causeway. We get in quickly and stand in the bows, whilst we silently cross the Landerneau river. It is a strange, mysterious boat-load; not a word is uttered, there is no sound but the heavy plodding and working of the oars, and the night is so dark we cannot see the faces of the men or the nature of the packages that weigh down the stern. The moon, rising through the clouds, just illumines the darkness as we near the shore; it shines on the smooth, wet mast, on the water-proof hat of the marine standing up in the boat, and reveals close to us the strong, stout arms of a girl, bared to the shoulder, her head concealed in a dark, tight-fitting headdress, with lappets like an Egyptian sphynx; the head is raised for a moment, and eyes are turned upon us as we leave, but no word is uttered, scarcely a " Bon soir!" as the boat drifts away into the night.

The moon shines as we ascend the hill—winding up a path between great rocks and under the shadow of stunted trees, to Plougastel — revealing a poor-looking town of plain stone houses, silent and deserted at this midnight hour. At a corner of two streets our companion points out the inn and takes leave, having to go to his home at the further end of the town. We knock for admittance, but without avail; heads are put out of various windows, but the answer is that every house is crowded, for "to-morrow is the fête"; and, truth to tell, curses are heaped upon the strangers for disturbing the dogs, who begin to howl as they trot by on their midnight errands. There is nothing to be done until daybreak, and so the night is spent in the open air.

We have come to Plougastel to see the people, and also its famous calvary, which stands in the middle of a desolate churchyard strewn with newly cut stone. As the day begins to dawn, we make our way to the church, and to the spot where we can just discern the calvary, with its carved figures . standing darkly against the sky. There is a flutter at our approach, for birds have been nestling behind the headless horsemen, and sheltering in the nooks and corners of the ancient pile. We leave them to silence a little longer, and stroll out to the highest ground to see the sun rise. Soon there is a streak of

light from the east, which gives shape and outline to the church
tower and the grey roofs of Plougastel, and, as we reach the high
ground outside the town, the landscape southward is lighting in the
morning sun; we see cultivated valleys and parklike views, with
pleasant green slopes leading down to the sea. But beautiful as is
the foreground, with its undulating green, interspersed with granite
boulders, with dew upon gossamer webs and little clouds of vapour
stealing between clumps of grass, the view across the bay, where the
distant headlands (indicated on the map overleaf) take a pearly
tinge, is the best sight of all. A little northward and westward are
the masts, chimneys, and church spires, and the smoke and steam,
of Brest, for the morning is breaking over a busy scene at the arsenal
and dockyards; but here, as the sun shines out, the sound in the
long grass are of grasshoppers, birds, and bees.

It is the morning of the fête; the thrush clears his throat, and
so do the peasants in their own way, as they come slowly up the
hill. Let us leave the view and go into the streets of Plougastel,
which are already alive with people, some of whom might be the
descendants of Eastern races, wearing Egyptian or Phrygian headdresses, caps from Albania, embroideries from Greece, and sashes from
Arabia. Here, then, for the first time in our travels, we find colour
predominating in the costumes of the people. Some of the women
wear close-fitting dark green caps embroidered with gold thread, their
dark skirts also bordered with embroideries or stripes of colour; some
wear white stockings and neat-fitting, red or black, slippers or shoes.
But the prevailing headdress of the women is the white cambric *coiffe*
with large side lappets and wide collars which we see elsewhere in
Finistère; the men have broad-brimmed hats with embroidered
strings or ribbons. Some of the men who come from the south
wear striped trousers with a red sash, and spare blue jacket with
numerous silver buttons, as in the sketch opposite. Some are dressed
entirely in blue cloth or serge, with sashes and red caps, but others
have broad white trousers and belts, their jackets and blouses
embroidered on the shoulders and sleeves. There is colour everywhere,

subdued by the dark blue of blouses and the sober brown and green
stuff gowns of the older women.

It is said that the people of Plougastel, preserving their old costumes
and traditions, still live much apart from their neighbours; a life half
seafaring, half agricultural, whose origin is traced to some early immi-

gration of Eastern races. By ten o'clock hundreds of people have come
in from the neighbouring villages, and as they all crowd together at
the church door and in the square round the calvary, we see the
strangest medley of costumes in all Brittany. They collect round the
calvary, some praying, some quarrelling or bargaining for small wares;
a general place of rendezvous on fête-days, especially on the 24th of
June (the Feast of St. Jean, called the "Pardon of Birds"), when

a large number of birds are offered for sale. This is a good day to see the costumes of the peasants, to hear their songs, and to see the dances in the streets of Plougastel.

The calvary was erected about the year 1602, and some of the figures are as sharp and clear as if carved yesterday; some are headless, and otherwise injured or destroyed. Around the three elevated crosses are a series of bas-reliefs, full-length figures cut in Kersanton stone, depicting various incidents in New Testament history—the Entry into Jerusalem, Christ teaching among the Doctors, the Offerings of the Magi, the Baptism of St. John, the Entombment, &c. On the south side is a representation of the Bearing of the Cross, on the north is the Judgment of Pilate, and so on. Some of the figures are very expressive, some have a certain quaintness and humour, and here and there we detect the same anachronisms in costume as at St. Thégonnec, where the Breton costume is introduced.

Altogether we must regard the calvary of Plougastel as a curiosity rather than as a great work of art; a grotesque group which, in its dark rugged outline set against the sky, will be remembered by travellers as something peculiar to Brittany, something which, in this land of strange mediæval monuments and relics, is yet perhaps the strangest sight of all.[*]

Returning to Daoulas, we join the high-road between Landerneau and Quimper, and pass southwards along the inland shores of the bay of Brest to Châteaulin. As travellers speed through this district by railway, they get glimpses, on the left hand, of the forest of Guimerch, and on the right, through the tree-tops, of inlets of the bay, and of the ancient little town of Le Faou, lying as it were at their feet.

On the railway we pass over an estuary at a great elevation, and on a greater part of the route to Châteaulin are on the spurs of the Monts d'Arrée. Travellers from Brest to Quimper should not be deterred from stopping at Châteaulin by the one line devoted to

---

[*] See sketch of a calvary on page 91.

it in guide-books, viz. "a dirty little town in parklike scenery, with no good inns."

The shores of the bay of Brest and the bay of Douarnenez are districts to be lingered in when the sun shines, for the days are really few when we may see the country to advantage. The luxuriance of foliage on the hills, the height of the grasses, the

deep green in the valleys, and the enormous umbrellas carried by the peasants, should remind us that fine days are few.

Châteaulin is crowded once a year to visit the Pardon of Ste. Anne la Palue, a ceremony that generally takes place on the last Sunday in August. The modern chapel of Ste. Anne stands alone upon high ground, overlooking the bay of Douarnenez, near Plonévez-Porsay, a small village about eight miles west of Châteaulin.

Crowds of people come from Brest by boat, and every road and pathway leading to the chapel is lined with people on the morning of the Pardon. The ceremonies are nearly the same as at Guingamp and at Ste. Anne d'Auray, but the camping-out of the people on the hillside above the sea (sometimes 10,000 in number), the processions of pilgrims, bare-footed, to the Holy Well of Ste. Anne, and other customs, are more curious than any to be seen elsewhere.

It is at the Pardon of Ste. Anne la Palue that the ceremonies of the church are rendered most picturesque from the surroundings, and where a greater variety of the ancient costumes of Cornouaille are to be seen. The trinkets, rosaries, and ribbons which are blessed and sold to the peasants are a modern importation from Angers or Lyons, but the embroidery round the dress of a beggar woman may be rare in colour and design. Nowhere else, excepting at Plougastel, shall we see such embroidered caps and bodices ; nowhere, not even at Auray, such bronzed and wrinkled human creatures.

The procession of the priests and people takes place on Saturday, about three in the afternoon, when the banner of Ste. Anne la Palue is carried across the hills by girls dressed in crimson, gold-embroidered robes, with scarves of silver thread and headdresses of lace and tissue of gold.

These are pictures in sunshine which are rare at Pardon times, and of summer nights when camping under tents is no hardship ; but what must the scene be at Ste. Anne la Palue in storm and rain, when thousands of pilgrims, old and young, have no shelter, when all colour and brightness has vanished, and the wind sweeps over the hills ?

Let us now turn inland a few miles, following the course of the Canal de Brest, to Châteauneuf du Faou, a small town where Mr. Caldecott made sketches at a Pardon which was held in the rain. This visit, made in 1874, will be best described in the artist's own words :—

"The courier for Châteauneuf du Faou left Châteaulin at 3 A.M. So we hire a phaeton, and proceed up the hilly road towards Pleyben. On the left is a beautiful vale with a pretty village by the side of

the river which runs towards Brest. The scenery is like the borders
of Wales, and the weather like that of Scotland; but the clean, elderly
girls coming down the road are like themselves only.

"We reach Pleyben in about two hours, a small deserted-looking
town with a wide *Place*, at one end of which is a curious calvary
(date 1670) undergoing repair, and an old church, partly Gothic,
partly Renaissance. The painted window over the altar is apparently

old, but part is replaced by plain glass. The ceiling is blue with gold
stars, and there are large painted effigies of the apostles in the porch.

"In about two hours after leaving Pleyben, the phaeton rattles
into the little town of Châteauneuf du Faou, knocking about the
umbrellas of the people crowding the streets on the occasion of a
pardon. The Hôtel du Midi, where we put up, is at the farther end
of the town, and is conducted in a simple manner. Ladies would not
like its arrangements. Several inhabitants, and a visitor or two, dine

at the table d'hôte, but all are unable to carve a duck except the English visitor, who is accordingly put down as a cook. There is music

in the streets, and the town is full of people, some of whom dance a kind of quadrille, called the 'gavotte,' in the market-hall; others attend a large booth to see acrobatic and other performances.

"The next day is still wet, and there are many people again in the streets, some from far away. The races come off on the high-road. I go to see the finish of one; four horses, strong and about fourteen hands high, gallop up a hilly length of a high-road; a pink, a red, a yellow, and a green and white jacket, dash by with a flourish of gaily tied up tails. I join the admiring crowd which encircles the winner, and we all go in procession to the Hôtel de Ville. I notice as the rider dismounts and enters the building to receive the prize (twenty francs) that he uses no saddle, wears his usual trousers, and has his coloured cap and jacket made of calico.

"In the large timber-built market-hall is a vast crowd of extensively linened, many-buttoned men—some with rosettes, the stewards of the fête—joined hand in hand in one long serpentine line with clean, red-faced, large-capped, big-collared girls. They jig along the earthen floor in shoes, clogs, and sabots to the music of a flageolet and a bag-pipe, varied by an occasional few bars of the voice. This is called the 'gavotte,' as the waitress of the hôtel, who is dancing, informs me. A farmer in blouse, with a collar (sketched overleaf), beats time with his sabots. One soldier, two town bonnets, and a few gendarmes relieve the costume of the peasants, which is, however, full of variety."

The Breton *ronde* or round dance, of which the gavotte is a good example, is one of the most characteristic scenes to be witnessed in

Brittany. At nearly every fête and gathering—in the streets, in the fields, or in the town-hall—we see the peasants dancing the gavotte, the musicians being generally two, one with the ancient Armorican bag-pipe (*biniou*), the other with a flageolet. Frequently, as in the sketch, one of the musicians puts down his instrument to sing.

The dancers keep good time, going through a variety of figures, but always returning to the *ronde*, dancing together, hand in hand, with great precision and animation, and a certain kind of grace. The gravity of manner and the downward look of the women in certain figures, as they advance and retire with hands down, give a peculiar quaintness to the gavotte, which, apparently rollicking and unrestrained,

is, in fact, orderly and regular in every movement. The circular motion of the dancers, now revolving in several circles, now in one *grande ronde*, is traced by M. Emile Souvestre, and other writers, to Druidic origin and the movements of the stars.

But as the dancers come swinging down the centre of the hall, hand in hand, now meeting, now parting; as fresh couples join and others fall into the rear; as we hear the measured tread and the voices which never seem to tire, we should be content to describe the "gavotte" as a good old country dance of singular animation and picturesqueness; a scene of jollity and at the same time of good order, of which the sketch gives an admirable idea.

There is one figure dressed in the latest fashion of Quimper, who is looked upon with doubtful admiration by the other dancers, but who will serve to remind us that distinctive costume, even in these out-of-the-way places, is a flickering flame, and that in a few years such scenes as the above will have lost their character.

We give a few bars of a favourite air, played with great spirit, which seemed to give the performers intense enjoyment, for they returned to it again and again.

At dusk oil lamps are lighted, a crowd fills the hall, and, when far
away down the wet streets of Châteauneuf du Faou, we can see the
steam rising between the rafters and hear the clatter of the dancers.

Four years later, on the 8th of August 1878, we arrive on a quiet,
sultry evening at the same little inn at Châteauneuf.   There is no
one in the house but two little children and some fowls, and the streets
are silent and almost deserted ; but at a little distance from the inn
we hear the heavy thud of flails, and going up a little green pathway
across the road, where a grey cloud of dust rises between the trees,

we come upon a scene of energy and determination which defies
description.   It is the last evening for threshing out a little patch of
corn, and the whole strength of the establishment has been enlisted
in the service, including the waiter, *chef de cuisine*, stable-boy, a farm
labourer, and one or two professional "batteurs" : four on one side, five
on the other, swinging and letting fall their heavy flails in turn, close
to each others' heads, with a precision and desperate energy wonderful
to behold.   Mr. Caldecott's sketches, taken at the moment, in a cloud
of dust, bring the scene before us most vividly ; the *garçon* of the inn,
the second in the row, all energy and excitement, putting his face

into his work so to speak, urging on the rest by shouts and gestures, but still keeping steady time with his flail; opposite to him, last but one, is "Madame," her face tied tightly over with a veil, as a protection from the dust; and, last in the line, the *chef de cuisine*, working as hard as the rest.

In the second sketch the leaders have changed position, the pace is quickened, and, from where we stand, the flails seem to fly dangerously close to the heads of the women. But no one flinches, and the strokes come down together as if from two operators instead of nine.

The grain is beaten out wastefully on the ground, and gathered into sacks by two old women, who put the straw afterwards into the pillows of the Hôtel du Midi.

CHAPTER VIII.

QUIMPER — PONT L'ABBÉ — AUDIERNE — DOUARNENEZ.

IN the fruitful valley of the Odet and the Steir, where two rivers join in their southern course to the sea, there rise the beautiful spires of Quimper, the present capital of Finistère; a town containing about 13,000 inhabitants, now the centre of the commerce and industry of southern Finistère, and, it may be added, the most pleasant resting-place on our travels. If we approach Quimper for the first time by road over the hills, we shall form the best idea of the beauty of its situation and of the picturesqueness of its buildings. The first impression of the traveller who arrives by train, and is hurried in an omnibus along the straight quays lined with trees, to the Hôtel de l'Épée, on the right bank of the river Odet, is one of slight disappointment at the modern aspect of the town; but let him glance for one moment from above out of one of the back windows of the inn (opened for him by the bright-faced maiden sketched on page 104), and the view of old roofs and cathedral towers will reassure his mind that neither in architecture nor in costume is this city likely to be wanting in interest. Quimper, the ancient capital of Cornouaille, with its warlike and romantic history of the middle ages, the centre of historic associations in the times of the War of the Success on, preserves many landmarks and monuments that will interest the traveller and the antiquarian. The fine Gothic cathedral has a richly sculptured porch with foliated carving of the fourteenth century, such as we saw at Le Folgoet. Above and between the two towers is an equestrian statue of the somewhat mythical King Gradlon, who held

a court at Kemper in the fifth century, whose prowess is recorded in the early chronicles of Brittany, and in the romances of the Round Table. The episode of his hunting in the neighbouring forests, being miraculously fed by one Corentin, a hermit, and finally converted to Christianity, is recorded continually in song and story : and from this incident (related by Souvestre and sung by Brizeux) dates the foundation of the ancient bishopric of St. Corentin. The statue, like nearly every monument in Brittany, was partly destroyed during the Revolution in 1793.

In spite of railways, telegraphs, and newspapers, and the bustle of commerce that fills the streets and market of Quimper, some of the inhabitants of the neighbouring valleys find time, on St. Cecilia's Day, to perform a pilgrimage to the cathedral and to sing songs in honour of St. Corentin. Thus we see how lovingly conservative Brittany clings to its monuments and legends, and how its people still dwell in the past. The story of King Gradlon may be a myth, but, like all legends and traditions, it has its origin in fact; and we who are not historians may be fascinated with the thought that the battered horseman, 'the object of so much interest to pilgrims in the past and to tourists in the present, is a link in a chain of facts, pointing backwards to a far-off time when, a little westward of the site of the present city of Quimper, on a promontory near Pont Croix, stood the ancient Celtic city of Is, remains of which are to be found to this day upon the shore.

The cathedral of Quimper was founded in the thirteenth century, but was principally built in the fourteenth and fifteenth. It has no very remarkable architectural features, but there is a grandeur in the lofty aspect of the interior, lighted by some fine stained glass, which leaves an impression of beauty on the mind. It is the centre and rallying-point for all the country round, the home of Catholicism, the "one church" to the inhabitants of Finistère. No picture of the wide *Place* by the river, where the great gatherings take place on fête-days, and where so many curious costumes are to be seen together, is complete without the two modern spires of the cathedral rearing high above the town. The procession of people passing up the wide street on a Sunday morning leading to its doors—a dense mass of figures, fringed with white caps, like foam on a heaving sea, the figures framed by projecting gables nearly meeting overhead—forms another picture which has also for its background the two noble spires.[*] The old houses in the market-place in the cathedral square, and the old inn, the Hôtel du Lion d'Or (this last well worthy of a sketch), are overshadowed by the pile. The people that come in by the old-fashioned diligences and the country carts and waggons go straight to the cathedral on arrival in the square.

The interior of the cathedral, which is the largest in Brittany, is very striking; there is a handsome chapel dedicated to Ste. Anne, the patron saint of Brittany, to St. Roch, and other saints. There is high-mass at half past ten, and a sermon by an ancient ecclesiastic preached from the handsome carved pulpit in the nave. It is an eloquent discourse, apparently, for along the aisles and between the pillars familiar-sounding phrases are poured fluent and fast. But the dense crowd of men and women with upturned faces on the pavement near the door can hear little of what is passing; the words take an upward curve of sound, and are heard more distinctly by the spiders and the flies. The loss may not have been great

---

[*] We believe it was to M. Viollet Le Duc, whose architectural taste and energy are so well known in France, that the completion of these towers is principally due.

if we take the testimony of a writer* in 1877, who says:—" I attended
mass one morning at Quimper, and the following is the substance
of a sermon preached to a large and attentive congregation mostly
of working men and women: 'There are three duties,' said the
preacher, 'imposed by the church on the faithful: first, to confess
at least once a year; secondly, to confess in one's own parish; thirdly,
to confess within the fifteen days of Easter.' The omission of the first
of these is regarded by the church as a sin of such gravity that

it is condemned to be punished by
the withholding of Christian burial.
Not one word, throughout a long
discourse to simple, devout, careworn
peasant folk, of moral teaching, religious counsel, or brotherly love!"

In some of the chapels there are
services during the day, and there is
a continual movement of white caps
in and out of the confessionals; and,
occasionally during the day, some
poor weather-worn man is doing
penance, going round and round the
cathedral on his knees, making a
curious slouching sound on the pavement (as grotesque a figure as

sketched on page 106). He is dressed in rags, and carries his sabots
under his arm during his long journey; thus, several times round the
pavement, dragging his weary limbs and—according to the enormity
of his sins—paying his sous as he goes.

The character of the people of this part of Cornouaille seems less
reserved, and there is a gay, genial aspect about them which is
refreshing when coming from the north. The bright face and figure
of the girl whose portrait Mr. Caldecott has caught exactly is one

---

* *A Year in Western France*, by M. Betham-Edwards.

of a flutter of five, who wait at table at the Hôtel de l'Épée in the
costume of the country, which, by the way, is worn here for the
especial benefit of travellers. It is probable that every one of these
bright-faced women would discard it to-morrow if they had the

chance (as their mistress and her children have done) ; but there is still
plenty of local costume to be seen in Quimper. We have only to
go out into the gardens, to visit the farms, by-roads, and lanes, and we
shall come upon some of the most picturesque scenes in our travels.

In the corner of a field just outside the town, where a lively
discussion is going forward between a farm labourer and three girls

at a well, there is a picture which for colour alone is worth remembering. It is one of those everyday scenes in which costume and the surrounding landscape harmonise delightfully. We give few sketches of architecture because photographs of the best examples may always be obtained, preferring rather to give the life of the

people. There are more figure subjects in the streets of Quimper than there is time to note. Thus, for instance, as we pass through a poor, dirty suburb at the lower end of the town, a woman comes to the door of a dark dwelling, and gives alms to a professional beggar, so grotesque and terrible in aspect that he hardly seems human; but the woman standing at the stone doorway wears a

costume that might have been copied from an Elizabethan missal.
She gives, as every one gives, to the poor in Brittany, but her
husband's small wages at the pottery works hard by leave little
margin for charity, and he will want all his spare money at this
time of year for the fêtes. The fêtes are an occasion for universal
feasting and rejoicing, in which the drinking propensities of the
holiday makers are only too apparent in the streets, leading in the

evening, sometimes, to domestic interviews like the one sketched
above.

At the time of the Fête of the Assumption there is a crowd at
Quimper from all parts of Finistère, and there is an amount of
festivity which must be bewildering to the quiet inhabitants; it is
then that we may see sometimes in the streets the splendid type
of Breton woman sketched at the head of this chapter, and, by
contrast, some others much more grotesque.

But perhaps the most interesting group of all, and the most complete and characteristic of Mr. Caldecott's sketches, is the one which forms the frontispiece to this volume—a scene in a *cabaret*, or wine-shop, where the farmers who have come in to market, whose carts we may see on the cathedral square, meet and discuss the topics of the day, amongst which, after the state of trade and the crops, the term of Marshal McMahon's government and the results of

the annual levy of "les conscrits" are uppermost. Soon after harvest-time, generally early in September, the annual levy of reserves for the army takes place, and Quimper, being the centre of a populous district, is the rallying-point for lower Finistére.

It is the nearest approach to an open political discussion that we may witness on our travels, and a good opportunity to see the conservative Breton farmer, the "owner of the soil," one who troubles himself little about "politics" in the true sense of the word, and is scarcely a match in argument for the more advanced republican trader and manufacturer of Quimper, but who, from hereditary instinct, if from no other motive, is generally an upholder of legitimist doctrines and a royalist at heart.

Seated on the carved oak bench on the left is a young Breton clodhopper or farm help, whose ill-luck it has been to be drawn this year; who leaves his farm with regret—a home where he worked from sunrise to sunset for two francs a week, living on coarse food and lodging in the dark with the pigs. As he sits and listens with perplexed attention to the principal speaker, and others gather round in the common room to hear the oracle, we have a picture which tells its story with singular eloquence, and presents to us the common everyday life of the people of lower Brittany with a truthfulness and vivacity seldom, if ever, exceeded. The only bright colour in the picture is in the red sashes of the men and in one or two small ornaments worn by the women.

Other scenes should be recorded if only to show, by way of
contrast, that Quimper is very like other parts of France. At one
of the *lycées* the annual prize-giving is going forward, and there is
a fashionable gathering, in which military uniforms are prominent. It
is an opportunity for seeing some of the *élite* of Quimper both on the

platform and in the crowded hall, and a great chance for a sketch.
The boys come up one by one, and stand on a raised platform to be
decorated with a paper wreath, to receive a book and a salutation on
both cheeks. It is interesting to note that, before joining his applaud-
ing friends in the hall, the boy takes off his wreath and throws it
away. There is scarcely a Breton costume in the hall.

In Quimper we are in a pleasant valley, surrounded by gardens, orchards, and fields, and sheltered from the wind by clustering woods.

The sun shines so warmly here that it is difficult to realise that a few miles to the west and south there are stretches of broad moorland leading to the boldest coast on the west of France. It is true that the people that come in from Pont l'Abbé, Audierne, and Douarnenez bear the impress of a seafaring life, and are different in style and costume to any that we have yet seen.

It is worth while for every one who stays in Quimper to see something of the coast, and to make a tour of at least two or three days to Pont l'Abbé, Penmarc'h, Pont Croix, the Pointe du Raz, and Douarnenez. In this short journey the traveller will see some of the finest coast scenery in Brittany, and people differing in character and costume from other parts of Finistère; a hardy fishing population, tempted to dangers and hardships by the riches to be found in the sea.

If the scenery which we have passed through on our way to Quimper resembled Wales, the district west of Quimper will remind us of Cornwall. We are, in fact, on the extreme edge of Brittany, corresponding to the Cornwall of England, *Cornouaille*, the *Cornu Gallia* of the ancients, a dangerous, storm-blown coast, wild, desolate, and picturesque. We may go down the river from Quimper to Pont l'Abbé, or a shorter route by road a distance of twelve miles, the first part over hills and through cultivated lands, in the latter part over wide moorland, covered with gorse and edged with pines. This is a beautiful drive, but, to judge of the quiet, almost mediæval stillness of Pont l'Abbé, it should be approached by water on a summer's evening, when, after a long and sometimes rather boisterous passage from the mouth of the river Odet, the little fishing-boat is rowed up the Pont l'Abbé river under the tower of its ancient castle. On the left, before entering the river, the little port of Loctudy is passed, where there is an ancient Romanesque church, well preserved, said to have been built by the Knights Templars in the twelfth century.

Pont l'Abbé with its dull, straight streets and deserted-looking houses, has no striking architectural features; but the costumes of

the people are altogether unique in Brittany, and the interiors of their dwellings are as quaint and curious as any painter would desire. The women wear close-fitting caps of red or green, embroidered with gold thread, the hair being turned up at the back and fastened at the top; they wear skirts of blue or green with a border of yellow, and the men, short blue jackets and sashes.

In Pont l'Abbé we may see, what is so rare in these days, an old street in which the costume of the people harmonises with the date

of the buildings, and in which the quiet of a past century seems never
to have been disturbed. Walk down a narrow grass grown street to
the open square above the river, at the end of which is the western
porch of the fine church of Pont l'Abbé, and the only two figures
visible in the afternoon are a girl carrying a basket coming from the
Carmelite convent, and a priest in black robes crossing the square.
The church and convent were founded in 1383, and there is little here
to mark the passage of years. The church has been completed and
beautified since those early times, and afterwards wrecked by the

Revolution; but the aspect of the square and of the cloisters of the
convent are little altered. The interior of the church is remarkable
for the grace and lightness of its pillars, and for the richness of its
stained glass; the rose windows are said to rival in beauty those
of Rouen. Notwithstanding that the church has but one aisle, that
the ceiling is now painted blue, and that the carvings in stone and
wood are sadly mutilated, it is an architectural monument of great
interest.

Six miles south-west of Pont l'Abbé, across a dreary, marshy
plain is the poor fishing town of Penmarc'h, built upon the dark,

rocks that form a barrier against the sea, on one of the wildest promontories of Cornouaille; a city whose riches in the fifteenth century were so great that, according to historians, " she could equip her three thousand men-at-arms, and shelter behind her jetties a fleet of eight hundred craft." The original prosperity of Penmarc'h arose from the cod-fisheries, which were the source of immense wealth before the discovery of Newfoundland. The history of its invasion by the English in 1404, and the disasters in the sixteenth century, when the town was partly destroyed by an inroad of the sea, and afterwards sacked by Guy Eder Fontenelle at the time of the Wars of the League, is one of the most romantic and terrible in the history of Brittany. It is a place to see if only to mark the traces of this wonderful city, once containing 10,000 inhabitants. A few ruined towers and the foundations of streets mark the site of the ancient city, which is now inhabited by a scattered fishing population numbering in all about 2000, the men braving the elements in their little fishing-boats, the women and children collecting seaweed and tilling the poor soil. There is a mass of rocks separated from the land, called the Torche de Penmarc'h, which all visitors are taken to see, and where the waves break upon the shore with the sound of thunder.

We have said little of the ruins of the church of St. Guénolé and of the parish church of Ste. Nonna at Penmarc'h, with its stained glass and quaint stone carving, or of other relics of the ancient city, because in nearly every town in Cornouaille there is some object of interest to examine. Antiquarian travellers should stay at the Hôtel des Voyageurs at Pont l'Abbé, where they will be very comfortably housed, and can explore this district, interesting not only for the historic associations connected with Penmarc'h, but for Druidical remains which the winds of the Atlantic are laying bare every year on this coast. It is a dreary, wind-swept promontory, from which the quiet superstitious inhabitants are only too glad to retreat. No wonder they flock into Quimper, and sun themselves on the *Place* during the summer days!

On the road between Pont l'Abbé and Audierne we obtain fine

I

views of the open landscape, with solitary figures here and there
working in the fields, and occasional glimpses of the sea. It is a
windy drive; the colour is sombre, and the clouds which come up in
heavy masses from the sea cast deep shadows over the land.

If we try to recall the impression of the scene, it is principally
of clouds, as in landscapes by Ruysdael or Géricault. The land for
miles is without sign of habitation, the highest point of interest is a
bank of furze, a stunted tree, or a heap of broken stones, chipped

perhaps from a fallen menhir; a solitude that seems more hopeless
and remote from the tumultuous aspect of the heavens.

But as we approach the town of Pont Croix, and, turning westward,
descend the hills to cross the estuary of Audierne, the view over the
bay is more luxuriant. Below us, through the stems of pine trees
that line the steep road, cut in granite rocks—as we descend to the
right bank of the river Goayen where it widens into an estuary—is
the little fishing village of Audierne, consisting of two or three straight
streets of granite houses, one or two large wharves and warehouses, a
lighthouse, and nearly a mile of protecting sea-wall. The evening is
now fine and calm, and the tide is coming in without a ripple, bringing

a few fishing-boats up to the quay, and attracting the inhabitants on to the *Place* in front of the principal inn, the Hôtel du Commerce, where the portly Père Batifoulier receives us, and provides us with excellent accommodation. It is a sheltered, sunny spot, surrounded by cultivated hills, where people come from Quimper to bathe in summer; but if we walk upon the downs behind the town, we shall get glimpses of a coast almost as exposed and dangerous to mariners as at Penmarc'h, where the sardine fishermen are spreading their nets on the grass.

Audierne is within six miles of the famous Pointe du Raz, the Land's End of Brittany, beyond which, stretching out into the Atlantic, is the Île de Sein, inhabited by a poor population of fishermen and seaweed gatherers. A glance at the map will show the position of the island, and the "Bec du Raz," the dangerous channel which divides it from the shore, through which the fishermen of Audierne and Douarnenez, with many prayers and crossings of the breast, pass and re-pass in their frail boats.

It is a dreary road from Audierne to the Pointe du Raz, passing the villages of Plogoff and Lescoff. At this point the rocks are higher above the sea than at Penmarc'h, and the scene is altogether more extensive and magnificent. We are on an elevation of eighty or ninety feet, and almost surrounded by the sea. To the south and east is the wide bay of Audierne, to the west the Île de Sein, the ancient home of Druidesses, and the horizon line of the Atlantic; to the north and east the bay of Douarnenez, across which is the jutting headland of La Chèvre.

A cloud of sea-birds rises from the rocks below, and floats away like a puff of steam, there is an orange tint in the seaweed piled upon the shore, and a purple tinge upon the distant hills across the bay of Douarnenez; but the green upon the scanty grass in the foreground is cold in colour, and almost the only flowers are yellow sea-poppies and the little white bells of the convolvulus. On every side are piles of rocks stretching out seaward as barriers against the waves of the Atlantic; a dangerous, desolate shore, on which many a vessel

I 2

has been wrecked. To the north is the Druids' "Baie des Trépassés," where, according to ancient legends, the spirits of the departed wait on the shore to be taken in boats to the Île de Sein. It is a Celtic legend, recounted in every history of Brittany.

The exposed position of the Pointe du Raz, the strange, fantastic grandeur of the rocks, and the wildness of the waves that beat upon the shore in almost all weathers, are alone worth a visit. The numerous artists who stay at Quimper, Douarnenez, and Pont-Aven, in the summer months would do well to pitch their tents for a time near the Pointe du Raz, if only to watch from this elevation the changing aspects of sea and sky, to see the sea, calm and blue in the distance, but dashing spray in sunshine over walls of rock, and

seaweed gatherers on a summer evening getting in their harvest, as deep in colour as the corn.

Leaving Audierne, and turning eastward towards Douarnenez, following the course of the river Goayen, we come in about an

hour to Pont Croix, an ancient town of 2500 inhabitants. The
church is a fine Romanesque building of the fifteenth century,
with a curious porch and some good carving in the interior. It is
a quiet, rather deserted-looking town, on an eminence above the
river, reminding one in its position and its air of faded importance
of the ecclesiastical city of Coutances, in Normandy.

It is a fine drive over undulating hills to Douarnenez, with views
of landscape more fertile than any we have seen since leaving Quimper ;
landscape with open moorland, interspersed with fields of corn, where

harvesting is being actively carried on, as in the sketch. Here we get a
glimpse of one of the old farmhouses of Finistère, and (on a very small
scale) of the farmer himself approaching in the distance to superintend
operations.

A few miles farther, and the landscape is again bare and unculti-
vated, we see peasants in the fields at rare intervals ; flocks of black
and brown sheep feeding on the open land. There is a charm of
wildness and a peculiar beauty about the scenery here that we who
write for artists should insist upon with all the power of the pen. It
is the fashion to stay at Douarnenez and at Pont-Aven, but we have
few records of the best scenery in Cornouaille.

Douarnenez, the headquarters of the sardine-fisheries, has a population of about 9000, almost entirely given up to this industry; the men in their boats, and the women and girls in the factories. It is a busy, dirty, and not very attractive town, with one principal street leading down to the port; but walk out of it in any direction, so as to escape the odours of the sardine factories, and the views from the high ground are most rewarding.

There is no prettier sight, for instance, than to watch the arrival of a fleet of several hundred fishing-boats rounding the last promontory, racing in whilst they are eagerly watched from the shore. At the point where the sketch was taken, the little fleet divides, to come to anchor at different inlets of the bay. Of the scene down at the port, where the boats unload; of the massing of a forest of masts against the evening sky, with rocks and houses high above as a background, we can only hint in these pages.

At Douarnenez, in summer, the inhabitants are accustomed to an inroad of visitors who come for the bathing season, and there is a little colony of artists who live comfortably at the principal inns (*en pension* for five or six francs a day), but it is not as quiet as Pont-Aven, of which we shall speak in the next chapter, for the streets are closely built and badly paved, and the busy inhabitants wear sabots which are rattled down to the shore at all hours of the day and night, according to the tide. Moreover, the inhabitants of the town are scarcely typical Bretons; they are a little demoralised by success in trade, a little inclined to smuggling, and decidedly fond of drinking. The men, living hard lives, facing the most fearful storms of the Atlantic in their exposed little boats, out sometimes for days without a take, are apt to be uproarious when on shore. The hardy, bright-featured women of Cornouaille, whose faces are becoming so familiar to us in these pages, have a rather sad and reckless look at Douarnenez; their homes are not too tidy as a rule; the little children play in streets which steam with refuse from the sardine factories, where their elder sisters are working in gangs, with bare feet and skirts tucked up to their knees, sifting, and sorting, and

WAITING FOR THE SARDINE BOATS AT DOUARNENEZ.

cooking sardines, and singing snatches of Breton songs the while.
The lower streets, steep and narrow, are blocked with fish-carts, and
the port is crowded with boats with nets drying in festoons. But
the view of Douarnenez seen at a little distance out at sea, with its
high rocks and overhanging trees almost reaching to the water's edge,
and above, the spire of the old church of Ploaré standing sharp against
the sky, will remain best in the
memory. There is no end to
the beauties of the bay of Douarnenez, if we explore the neighbourhood, starting off early for
the day and not returning until
sundown.

In the evening there is a great
Bohemian gathering at the Hôtel
du Commerce; its artistic visitors
overflow into the street, and make
themselves heard as well as seen.
There is a clatter of tongues and
a cloud of smoke issuing from
the little café presided over by
the neat figure in the sketch.
Those who have been to the
Hôtel du Commerce at Douarnenez will recognise the portrait
at once; those who have not
must picture to themselves a girl
with dark hair and brown complexion, a headdress and bodice in
which scarlet and gold are intermingled, a dark skirt with a border
of yellow or orange, and a spotless white apron and sleeves. In soft
shoes she flits silently through the rooms and supplies our clamorous
wants in turn; neither remonstrance nor flattery will move her, or
cause her to raise her eyes.

The children of Douarnenez have learned to beg, and along the

broad road which leads to Quimper, beggars are stationed at intervals
to waylay the charitable. Driving home in the little covered carriage
shown in the sketch, a dark object appears before us on the way.
Near it, at the side of the road, is a little shed roughly made with
poles and brambles, and, protruding from it, two sabots filled with
straw, two sticks, and a pair of *bragous bras*. The rest of the structure
consists of dried ferns, and a poor deaf human creature propped up
to receive the alms of the charitable, a grim figure watching and
waiting in the sun and wind.

CHAPTER IX.

CONCARNEAU — PONT-AVEN — QUIMPERLÉ.

FOURTEEN miles south-east of Quimper is Concarneau, another important fishing station of Cornouaille. It is well to go thither by road, in order to see the view of Quimper and the valley below, when a few miles out of the town; a view which few travellers see in these days. The old town of CONCARNEAU, with its fortifications and towers, called "Ville Close," which in its position somewhat resembles St. Malo, is approached by a drawbridge from the mainland, and at high tide is surrounded by water; it consists of one long irregular street with old houses shut in by dark walls, through the loopholes of which we see the sea. The nominal population of Concarneau is 5000, but in the Faubourg Ste. Croix, where the fleet of fishing-boats come and go at every tide, the population is upwards of 10,000. There is a fine modern aquarium, and there are several interesting monuments in the immediate neighbourhood, but there is nothing very remarkable in the situation of the town itself, and it is certainly not a place for visitors to stay in; the work of life at Concarneau is to catch and cure little fishes, and the odours of the dead and the dying, the cured and the fried, pervade the air. The hedges are made of the cuttings of sardine boxes.

We happen to see Concarneau at its best on a fine summer's morning, when the wide quay of the Faubourg Ste. Croix, where

the sketch is taken, is alive with people, the majority on their way
to church across the drawbridge in the Ville Close. The little fleet
of fishing-boats is moored in a cluster at the quay; the nets are
drying in the sun *en masse*, and the cork floats hang from the masts

in graceful festoons. Everyone is in holiday attire, and seems bent
upon going somewhere—to church, for a drive in the country, or for
an excursion out to sea. The fishermen and workmen have for the
most part disappeared into the wine-shops, whence their hilarity over-

Checkmate at Sunday morning

flows into the streets. The girls employed in the sardine factories
have put on their best dresses and neatest shoes, and go in companies
of six or eight together to the church. Their smooth white caps and
lappets glisten in the clear air which blows lightly from the south-
east, and the odours of sardines are for the time forgotten. It is the
time and the spot from which to take away an impression of Concarneau, for its ordinary every-day aspect is not romantic. The

procession of people coming from church down the old-fashioned
street, shut in by walls and towers, makes a good picture. The
majority wear their proper costume, as sketched on opposite page;
a few only have fallen into temptation, and carry bonnets, trains,
and high heels across the *Place*.

There is a wide, open space in front of the Hôtel des Voyageurs,
on the quay Ste. Croix—where, at a window overlooking the quay,
the *femme de chambre* is putting the last touches to her toilet—but
behind it are narrow, dirty streets, crowded cafés and estaminets, where

On the Quay at Concarneau.

the husbands of these white-capped women have disappeared for the
day. The majority of the well-to-do . inhabitants are *en promenade*
under the trees, and nearly everyone is bent upon pleasure of some
sort. Here is a party just starting for a boating excursion across the
bay, singing a Breton air to the time of the rowers, which we can
hear on the quay. The sketch gives the exact picture: the heavy

fishing-boat built for rough weather and stormy seas; the rowers
standing four abreast, the heavy ears plashing in the sunlight, the
boat down at the stern with its holiday load; whilst the *gamin* of
Concarneau sits on the edge of the quay, over the principal drain of
the town, with a string to catch little fishes.

The sketch on the quay when the tide is out, with people
waiting for the ferry-boat, gives the aspect looking seaward, on a
quiet evening, as we drive away towards PONT-AVEN.

To reach Pont-Aven, we ascend and descend some gently sloping hills, in an easterly direction, for about eight miles. On the left hand of the road, near the village of Trégunc, we pass one of the largest rocking stones in Brittany, a block of granite 12 feet long by 9 feet,

poised upon a second slab half buried in the ground. Little children lie in wait for travellers, and move this stone, which is known far and wide as "La pierre aux maris trompés," a stone by which husbands are said to test the fidelity of their wives. All the heath-covered land on the way to Pont-Aven is strewn with granite boulders; there is a celebrated dolmen, or "table stone," in the neighbourhood, and, near at hand, at Rustéphan, are the picturesque remains of a fifteenth-century castle, which may be reached through a wood by leaving the road at the village of Nizon, two miles from Pont-Aven.

At a point where the river Aven—breaking through its narrow channel, dashing under bridges and turning numerous water-wheels—spreads out into a broad estuary, is the little port of Pont-Aven, built four miles from the sea. The majority of the houses are of granite, and sheltered under wooded hills; the water rushes past flour-mills and under bridges with perpetual noise, and a breeze stirs the poplar trees that line its banks on the calmest day. The widest part of the village is the *Place*, sketched (looking northwards) from the stone bridge which gives Pont-Aven its name. A small community of farmers, millers, fishermen and peasant-women, is its native population, supplemented in summer by a considerable foreign element.

Pont-Aven is a favourite spot for artists, and a *terra incognita* to

the majority of travellers in Brittany. Here the art student, who has spent the winter in the Quartier Latin in Paris, comes when the leaves are green, and settles down for the summer to study undisturbed. How far he succeeds depends upon himself; his surroundings are delightful, and everything he needs is to be obtained in an easy way that will sound romantic and impossible in 1879. Pont-Aven being set in a valley between two thickly wooded hills, opening out southwards to the sea, the climate is temperate and favourable to out-door work. In the centre of the village is a little triangular *Place*, and at the broad end, facing the sun, is the principal inn, the Hôtel des Voyageurs, which, at the time of writing, has an excellent hostess, who takes *pensionnaires* for about five francs a day, "tout compris," and where the living is as good and plentiful as can be desired. This popular hostelry is principally supported by American artists, some of whom have lived here all through the year; but many English and French painters have stayed at Pont-Aven, and have left contributions in the shape of oil paintings on the panels of the *salle à manger.*

We have mentioned the Hôtel des Voyageurs; but there are other inns; there is the Hôtel du Lion d'Or, also on the *Place*, frequented principally by French artists and travellers; and down by the bridge, a quaint little auberge (with a signboard painted by one of the inmates), the Pension Gloanec. This is the true Bohemian home at Pont-Aven, where living is even more moderate than at the inns. Here the panels of the rooms are also decorated with works of art, and here, in the evening, and in the morning, seated round a table in the road, dressed in the easy *bourgeois* fashion of the country, may be seen artists whose names we need not print, but many of whose works are known over the world. The resources of these establishments are elastic, accommodation being afforded, if necessary, for fifty or sixty *pensionnaires*, by providing beds a few yards off in the village. The cost of living, board and lodging, at the Pension Gloanec, including two good meals a day with cider, is *sixty francs* a month! When we add that the bedrooms are clean

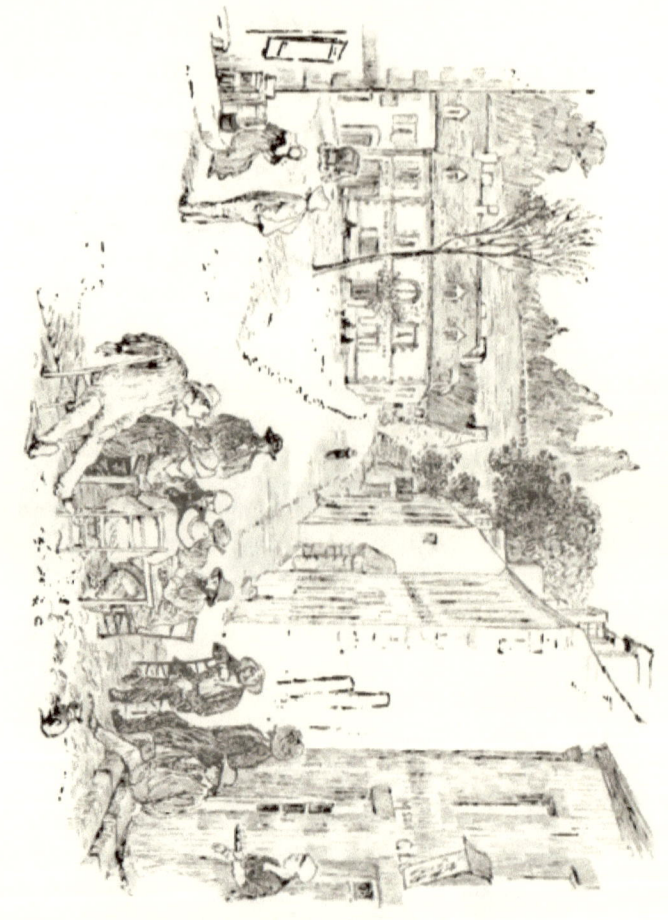

PONT-AVEN.

and bright, especially those provided in the neighbouring cottages, we
have said enough about creature comforts, which are popularly supposed to be unknown in Brittany. The materials for work and
opportunities for study are similar to those in Wales, with fewer
distractions than at Bettws-y-Coed.

At Pont-Aven the presiding genius at the Hôtel des Voyageurs
is one Mademoiselle Julia Guillou. At this little inn, as at the Hôtel
du Commerce at Douarnenez, the traveller need not be surprised to
find that the conversation at table is of the Paris *Salon*, to find
bedrooms and lofts turned into studios, and a pervading smell of oil
paint. It is said of Pont-Aven that it is "the only spot in Europe
where Americans are content to live all the year round"; but perhaps
the kind face and almost motherly care of her *pensionnaires* by the
portly young hostess, Mademoiselle Julia Guillou, has something to
do with their content.

The views in the neighbourhood of Pont-Aven are beautiful, and
the cool avenues of beeches and chestnut trees, a distinctive feature
of the country, extend for miles. From one of these avenues, on the
high ground leading to an ancient chapel, there is a view over the
village where we can trace the windings of the river far away towards
the sea, and where the white sails of the fishing-boats seem to
pass between the trees. The sides of the valleys are grey with
rocks, and the fields slope steeply down to the slate roofs of the
cottages built by the streams, where women, young and old, beautiful
and the reverse, may be seen washing amongst the stones.

Pont-Aven has one advantage over other places in Brittany; its
inhabitants in their picturesque costume (which remains unaltered)
have learned that to sit as a model is a pleasant and lucrative
profession, and they do this for a small fee without hesitation or
"mauvaise honte." This is a point of great importance to the artist,
and one which some may be glad to learn through these pages.
The peasants, both men and women, are glad to sit for a franc for
the greater part of a day; it is only at harvest time, when field
labourers are scarce, that the demand may be greater than the supply.

RETURNING FROM LABOUR, PONT-AVEN.

and recruits have to be found in the neighbouring fishing villages. Once or twice a week in the summer, a beauty comes over from Concarneau in a cart, her face radiant in the sunshine, the white lappets of her cap flying in the wind. Add to these opportunities

for the study of peasant life and costume the variety of scenery, and the brightness and warmth of colour infused into everything under a more southern sun than England, and it will be seen that there are advantages here not to be overlooked by the painter.

The picturesque town of QUIMPERLÉ on the rivers Ellé and Isole, from which so many English travellers have been scared, in years gone

by, by Murray's laconic admonition, "No good inn," is a most pleasant
and comfortable resting-place. It is approached on a high level
when coming by railway from Quimper, the road from the station
winding round the hills down to the *Place*, where there is the comfortable Hôtel des Voyageurs. On arriving at Quimperlé, the aspect
of the people is more cosmopolitan, for we are approaching the
borders of the province of Morbihan, and are on the highway between
Nantes and Brest.

at Quimperlé Station

The people at the station are not numerous, and they are nearly
all third-class travellers. The quiet, almost taciturn company consists
of a tourist, a *sergent de ville*, a commercial man of Quimperlé, the
same old woman that we meet everywhere on our travels, in the comfortable dark hood and cape of the country, and a peasant-woman
taking home her sack of meal, sketched on the opposite page.

Quimperlé contains about 6500 inhabitants, principally occupied
in agriculture. It is surrounded by hills covered with orchards
and gardens shut in by high walls; an old and sleepy place,
full of memories of the past, and with, apparently, little ambition
for the future. There is an ancient abbey church, built in the

eleventh century, on the plan of the Holy Sepulchre at Jerusalem; in the crypt is the tomb of St. Gurloës, one of the early abbots of Quimperlé. The large grey-roofed building on the *Place* adjoining this church, now used as the Mairie, was formerly a convent of

Benedictine nuns; and other buildings, such as the old inn, the Lion d'Or, were originally used by the abbots of St. Croix.

But Quimperlé, in spite of its railway, is a town where grass grows between the paving-stones of its streets; a place which owes much of its attraction to its picturesque site and its ancient buildings, to its market-days, its weddings and fêtes. In the lower town there are some old narrow streets, with most picturesque wooden gables, and there is one dilapidated square, called "the Place of Revolution," where there would seem little left to destroy.

A painter might well make Quimperlé a centre of operations, for its precincts are little known; the gardens shine with laden fruit-trees, and the hills are rich in colour until late in autumn; and in the evening there is no better place for rest than under the trees on the Place Nationale. Here the people pass to and fro, as in

the sketch on the opposite page; there are more women than men to be seen, for the latter are resting from their labours, in the cafés. Beyond, and high above this group, are the houses of the old town, surmounted by the two square Gothic towers, with spires covered with lichen, of the church of St. Michel. Under the trees near the river are women selling sardines and fruit. The position of the bridge over the Ellé is indicated by the man leaning over the stone parapet. The man with the cart has just come in with wood for winter fires.

The great attraction to Quimperlé is in the country round; in the beauty of the woods and the windings of the streams. In this

On the Place at Quimperlé

neighbourhood the artist and the angler may settle down together
and spend the summer months delightfully.

We said that Quimperlé, a town with a railway station, on the
great highway between Nantes and Brest, owes most of its life and
picturesque attraction to women, weddings, fêtes, and flowers. Let us
picture a prominent personage at the old Hôtel du Lion d'Or. She
had a beautiful name, *Augustine*, pronounced with enviable accuracy

A BIG LOAD

by all the household. She hovered about us like a fairy, attend-
ing to our wants in the most delicate way; to outward seeming a
ministering angel with pure white wings, but, in truth, a drudge, a
methodical housewife, massive, and hard to the touch. She did the
work of three Parisian *garçons*, and walked upstairs unaided with port-
manteaus which it would require two men to lift, anywhere out of
Brittany. She slept in a box in the kitchen, and dressed " somehow "
in five minutes. She ate what was left, contentedly, at the end of
the day, and rose at sunrise to do the laborious work of the house ;

helping also at harvest-time in the fields. She had the sweetest of smiles (when she liked), an unconquerable habit of taking snuff, and a murderous way of killing fowls in the early morning which we shall not easily forget.

How it comes to pass that this girl of nineteen occupies such an important position in the household is one of those things which are peculiar to Brittany. The strong individuality, industry, and force of character of the women make themselves felt wherever we go. Whilst the men slumber and smoke, the women are building little fortunes or propping up old ones. All through the land, in the houses, in the factories, and in the fields, the strong, firm hand and arm of a woman *does the work.*

The pedestrian or sportsman, in his wanderings through Brittany, will, if he knows the country, seek, at the end of a long day, the country *auberge* where a "household fairy" presides. The land is full of legends and tales of gnomes and witches, but the reality is a white-capped figure, that welcomes the traveller at the inn door the modern

AUGUSTINE.

representative of "mine host." Her brightness and attraction, and at the same time her whole armour and coat of mail, are her stiffly starched cap, epaulets, and apron of spotless white. She presides at the fêtes and weddings which are celebrated at the inns, and joins in the frolics at the end of the day, dancing with the rest up and down the street, and submitting with modest but hearty goodwill to some rather demonstrative tokens of esteem. "How is it that these widespread collars are never crumpled?" some one asks. "Oh, we just turn them round and throw them over the shoulder for a minute!" is the quick answer.

Let us refer to our notebook to see how one of these weddings is managed in Quimperlé in 1878. It is just after harvest, and the time for rest and festivity in many a village round. Coats and gowns that have been laid by for months are brought out, and many an antique-shaped garment sees the light for the first time for a year. Two or three weddings are arranged for the same day, and at early morning all meet at Quimperlé. The girls come on foot, dressed in their local costumes, excepting a little innovation of finery here and there ; the " boys," for they are little more in age, have modernised themselves, and wear a clumsy imitation of the conventional suit of black, being especially proud of Parisian hats. But excepting in the matter of costume, they do as their forefathers did ; they spend the day in the streets of Quimperlé, parading arm-in-arm with their brides, stopping to take, and to give, refreshment at every inn-door and at the homes of all their friends. We meet them early in the morning crossing the principal square ; they have registered their marriages, and have taken the sacrament in the church of St. Michel, in the upper town, and for the rest of the long summer day and half into the night they dance the "De Rober" up and down the streets, hand in hand together, to the music of the bagpipe and the flageolet.

CHAPTER X.

HENNEBONT.

FROM Quimperlé to Hennebont by road or railway, we pass Pont Scorff, where is the boundary line which divides the departments of Finistère and Morbihan. We enter now the district of Bas-Bretagne, the Arcadia of Brittany, of which so much has been written and sung by French writers, and of which only those who have lingered in its by-ways have discovered the charm. It is the part of Brittany most interesting from its historic associations, the land most strewn with dolmens and menhirs, and mysterious Druidical remains.

Holiday travellers from Quimper to Vannes pass by the large and busy town of L'Orient because it is described, truly, as " an uninteresting modern town with straight streets and quays," and many also pass by HENNEBONT. There is no historic interest in L'Orient, whose 40,000 inhabitants are busy in shipping and trade—the trade, amongst other things, of importing foreign spirits and tobacco, and of planting in every village in Brittany the cheap manufactured cottons and fineries which stamp out individuality in costume, the last stronghold of self-respect amongst the peasants, both men and women. In every remote village, on church walls and on mediæval towers, is posted in glowing colours the announcement of a **Grand Magasin des Modes** at L'Orient, and every afternoon there comes by train to Hennebont the *Petit Journal* to complete the work of civilisation ; a little journal, distributed by hand to all who possess a sou, giving in its daily sheet little beyond Parisian gossip, but containing sometimes some strange paragraphs like the following, which would seem of doubtful interest to Bretons :—

"— On adoucit les maris et on les habitue à des mouvements aristocratiques."

"— On communique aux jeunes ladies le nom et la profession de leur futur mari."

"— On enseigne l'élégance et la grâce en douze heures, succès garanti."

"— On loue et on échange de petits enfants."

"— On coupe les oreilles et la queue aux chiens d'après la dernière mode."

Hennebont is only five miles from L'Orient, and of course some of the inhabitants wear the modern dress, but it is still very primitive-looking, being seldom visited by strangers. Sloping southward towards the river, where ships are loading and unloading at the little port, is the chief street, shown in the sketch opposite. Hennebont is an old historic town, containing about 5000 inhabitants, and is the natural outlet for the produce of the surrounding country. At the upper end the street widens into a grass-grown *Place*, where is the church of Notre Dame de Paradis, with its square tower and lofty recessed portal, the

work, it is believed, of an English architect in the sixteenth century, a structure not in any way very remarkable. The town is divided into the comparatively modern Ville Neuve, sketched above, the Ville Close, and the Vieille Ville on the right bank of the Blavet, memorable for its sieges in the War of Succession in Brittany, and for the exploits of the Countess of Montfort in defending the city

I.

in the fourteenth century, of which Froissart gives a spirited account in his Chronicles.

In the high-street of the town, the Ville Neuve, are the two principal inns, we can hardly call them hotels, outside one of which a traveller reposes after the midday meal; and a little below are the

older hostelries, where there have been numerous arrivals during the day. Opposite, or a low wall, is a shelter of trees, a favourite lounge, whither come in the afternoon the old and the young to talk, to quarrel, and to flirt.

Sit down on the wall and watch the passers by. First a cart, drawn by diminutive bullocks, heavily laden with field produce, comes

REAPERS ON THE ROAD.

lumbering down, the driver in broad-brimmed hat and heavy sabots; next, a clatter of hoofs and a troop of high-bred horses, led or ridden by riders in scarlet coats and white trousers, pass down to the river; they come from the *haras* in the neighbourhood, one of the government breeding establishments; this gives a dash of colour and a style to Hennebont quite foreign to its ordinary aspect. Next, with heavy, measured tread, comes a procession, half solemn, half grotesque, of reapers and professional *batteurs* changing their quarters. Next

comes out and stands at the door of the Hôtel de France the inn-keeper, dressed, unlike most of his neighbours, in a frock-coat and hat; a slim man in dandy Parisian attire, almost the only black figure to be seen in Hennebont.

Women pass busily up and down, carrying heavy loads, some with the white lappets of their caps thrown backward, treading heavily like beasts of burden. Excepting for a short time in the heat of the day, when the men rest and the women knit, there are few unemployed hands in Hennebont.

The evening brings more activity, the farmers and their wives pack
up and depart in their country carts, shutters open in the dark grey-
stone houses on the *Place* near the church ; the *maire* and the *avocat*
take a walk, or a drive with their families : and women and children
emerge on various errands. It is then that out of side streets, and

doorways in walls unlocked with heavy keys, issue, one by one, the
fairest inhabitants of Morbihan, some especially erect, bearing earthen
vessels on their heads, wending their way up the town to a road beyond
the church, where, under the cool shade of trees, and partly shut in by
walls, is the fountain which supplies Hennebont with water. It is a
rendezvous for old and young, men, women, and cattle, a place to see
and to sketch, charming in its sheltered aspect after a midday sun ;

women coming and going with their pitchers; men helping or bringing
cattle to water, and numerous washing parties on their knees.

Every way we turn there is a picture of some sort to be sketched;
if we follow the narrow, winding streets of the Ville Close, sheltered

by trees and overshadowed by walls, we come suddenly upon an old
time-stained doorway like that below; and, amongst the people that
crowd the poorer quarter, are many quaint and interesting groups.

Here we may notice again the harmonious combinations of
costume and buildings, and how the women, tall and straight, clad
in draperies of soft material, seem to give dignity to the most
squalid surroundings.

They are a pleasant, homely people at Hennebont; a town worth visiting before simplicity, individuality, and local costume have passed away.

But the air is close in this valley, and we are too near the main line of railway; let us turn northward to see something more of the interior of the province of Morbihan.

CHAPTER XI.

LE FAOUET — GOURIN — GUÉMÉNÉ.

IT is a pleasant change, even from the quiet of Hennebont, to wind slowly up the hills covered thickly with ferns and woods, to disturb the magpies on the roads, and the yellow-hammer and the lizards on the rough stone walls; to see the silent peasants knee-deep in the fields, the little black and white cattle tethered to pasture, the black and brown sheep grazing in the open land, and the pigs at the cottage doors. It is a considerable ascent from the town through an undulating landscape of woods and streams and ferns; the valleys green in their depths, the trees turning gold and brown where they fringe the hills.

As we approach Le Faouet, the scene changes gradually to a sterner aspect, the trees are less luxuriant, and the soil is less fruitful. Here and there we pass on the road a busy harvest scene, the people turning round at the sound of approaching wheels to watch the travellers pass. It is the farmer himself that gazes at us, half amused; the time for harvest is short on these rainy hills, and so master and man, and every available help, work early and late to get in the crops. The sun that shines so brilliantly to-day, and lights up the harvest field with a golden glow, will disappear in a few hours, and the fields may be a wreck from the wind and rain. Every now and then a deep shadow is thrown over the land from the clouds that drift eastward from the sea, but they are high in the

REAPING NEAR HENNEBONT.

heavens to-day, and the sky is of an almost Eastern blue. Before us northwards the horizon is of a colder hue, and as we ascend the last long hill to Le Faouet, the cupola on the church tower and the grey roofs of the houses with their backgrounds of firs have by contrast a sombre tinge.

On the road from Quimperlé to Le Faouet a stream is crossed that divides the two provinces of Finistère and Morbihan; it is a stream well stocked with trout; in fact, in most of these rivers there

is excellent fishing, and there are no better headquarters for sport than Le Faouet. The town, which is well situated and has fine views of the country, contains not more than 3000 inhabitants, nearly all but the oldest and the poorest being engaged in agriculture. It is a great centre on certain days, when the people collect under the eaves of the market-place shown in the full-page sketch.

But excepting the visits of a few sportsmen and tourists in summer, Le Faouet is scarcely ever visited by the outer world. The houses are built of stone, old and covered with lichen; the covered market-place has heavy wooden eaves, and is protected by ancient elms ; the inhabitants are dressed for the most part in rough and primitive fashion, the men in white cloth jackets, loose breeches, and sabots, and the women in dark comfortable cloth hoods, as in the sketch at the head of this chapter.

It is a quiet, self-contained, dignified population at Le Faouet, approached at intervals by the commercial traveller, and a few cattle- and horse-dealers, but holding otherwise little communication with towns. Here, in this neighbourhood, we may contemplate the typical Breton, who, braced physically to withstand the shocks of the tempest, resists with an almost irresistible *vis inertia* the advance of French civilisation ; whom neither the progress of steam nor compulsory education has much disturbed. He has, for trading purposes, acquired some knowledge of French, but he keeps this knowledge to himself, and never displays it unnecessarily ; he has thus an advantage over strangers, who may imagine he cannot understand a word.

To come into a quiet village like Le Faouet with no purpose but observation requires a certain amount of courage, and, if it were not

that a little more than a mile north of Le Faouet there is the famous chapel of Ste. Barbe, and southward about two miles, in an old church, there is an elaborately carved rood-screen, we might hesitate to take up our quarters here. Unless a man has business in Le Faouet unless he is an antiquary, a fisherman, or a painter, he would leave it the day he entered. It is not, however, uncommon for the landlord of the Hôtel du Lion d'Or to have *pensionnaires* who stay for the summer.

In spite of the grandeur of its situation, the solidity of its buildings, and the evident industry of the inhabitants, there is a dreary, ruinous look about the *Place* of Le Faouet even on a summer's day. What must it be in winter winds? On the brightest and driest day of the year many of the houses are dark and unhealthy-looking, built close together, with narrow lanes of mud and filth between them. What must they be when the rains begin?

We have seen in Le Faouet some of the finest types of Bretons, both men and women. Let us record one figure which will never be

effaced from memory. Passing down a street leading from the
principal square, we meet coming up the hill bareheaded, in the full
blaze of the sun, in the dust and heat, the strange, wild-looking
figure in the sketch ; his clothes are patched, his hair is white, his
face red ; with crutches, and one leg, he drags (with the help of a
dog and one or two charitable children) his house, with him about

the town. It is a strange conveyance made of sticks and dried
ferns, but it is *home.* Travellers see strange sights, but surely no
sight more grotesque was ever seen than "the man on two sticks"
of Le Faouet, whose portrait is given to the life.

Before leaving Le Faouet, a visit should be made to the fifteenth-
century church of St. Fiacre, to see the fine rood-screen elaborately
carved with figures representing scenes in the life of Christ, panels

of elaborate and grotesque workmanship. The work on this screen was partly executed in 1480 and in 1627, and the whole was restored, painted, and gilt in 1866. There is also some fine stained glass, dating from 1552.

To the chapel of STE. BARBE is a shaded walk of about a mile and a half—first through narrow lanes and broad avenues, then up a steep ascent where the path is sometimes cut in steps in the rock. It brings us in half an hour to a high plateau fringed with furze and wind-blown pines. The view from the eminence is magnificent: the eye wanders eastward and southward, over a broad valley with a mountain stream, the Ellé winding first through beds of rocks, then into pastures, and disappearing in cultivated fields. As we walk to the edge of this mountain-side, where there is only a small hut visible, the panorama increases in extent over the country, and the variety of colour, from the grey of scattered boulders and blue of pines, to the deep green of the meadows and woods, forms a scene of such natural beauty that we almost forget the object of our mission.

The chapel of Ste. Barbe, approached down a flight of steps, is actually close to our feet; it is built of granite under the hillside, sheltered from the winds by enormous rocks and trees, and with a steep declivity below; a solid granite structure fitted into the hillside, so to speak, the space not permitting the nave of the chapel to be in the usual position. In the interior—which is shown by an old man in tatters who kneels at the altar whilst we walk round—is a gallery with carved panels, supported by seraphim holding shields, and grotesque animals on the mouldings; there is also some old stained glass.

There is a tradition attaching to this chapel, that a knight, hunting in the neighbourhood in the fifteenth century, was overtaken by a storm in the valley below, and, being preserved from falling rocks by the prayers of Ste. Barbe, erected this chapel to her memory. From that day there has been an annual pilgrimage to Ste. Barbe, when some of the devotees creep round the precipitous exterior walls as an act of penance. Before leaving, we pass up the rough stone

steps in the sketch to even higher ground, where there is a small
chapel dedicated to St. Michel.   It is fortunate to have seen the
view from Ste. Barbe on a clear day, for the clouds, which gather
in the distance, as white as snow, through the tree tops, come up in
a few hours and shroud the land.

Ten miles in a north-westerly direction, in some of the finest
scenery of the Montagnes Noires, is GOURIN, a small town in the
centre of a district of old iron mines, stone and slate quarries.   Mr.
Caldecott, who visited this district in a previous year, in bad weather,
speaks of the "wide, dirty, uninteresting-looking street of Gourin, at
the top of which is the Hôtel du Cheval Blanc," but he has
made a sketch of the women washing at a stream just outside the

town, which only wants colour to be one of the m st picturesque of our series.

Excepting for fishing, shooting, or perchance to record the forms and colours of the mountains in a sketch, few visitors will find their

way to Gourin, even in summer; but the following notes by the artist may be interesting to travellers :—

"The dining-room of the inn at Gourin opens on to the public *Place*, and is frequented by commercial travellers and two or three residents ; one of the latter, being a *chasseur*, is followed through the glass door by a pack of hounds, the large sporting spaniels of the country, and at each guest's elbow a dog stations himself to receive gratuities."

M

"After resting for the night in a comfortable room, separate from the main premises, I hire a vehicle to take me to Le Faouet, as the morning is wet; a long-bodied cart, drawn by a white horse, with the wheels set forward and a shifting seat, on which is a large pillow. We drive through a hilly, wooded country in a high wind."

The storm is so severe at Le Faouet that "slates are blown

"MONTEZ, S'IL VOUS PLAIT, MONSIEUR!"

from the roofs of the houses, men grasp their hats, women tack hither and thither across the square, and geese take advantage of the breeze and try to fly." On the way to Ste. Barbe, "a tall tree crashes across the path, which is strewn with unripe acorns, chestnuts, apples, fir cones, leaves, and twigs."

The hurricane that was experienced here swept over the whole of Brittany with great violence, and, according to the *Journal de Rennes*, "laid low at least a thousand trees."

Up and down again on a good road, a drive of seventeen miles from Le Faouet takes us to GUÉMENÉ, meeting a few reapers, and a cart drawn by bullocks in charge of men who have succumbed to thirst and heat.

We halt halfway at the poor village of Kernascléden, where there is hardly an inhabitant to be seen, but where, abutting on the high-road, is a beautiful Gothic church, rich in carving and grand in proportion, a striking contrast to the hovels which immediately surround

it. It is a good example of fifteenth-century work, built at the same time as the church of St. Fiacre, and by the same founder. There is a legend here too curious not to repeat, that angels aided in the building of these two beautiful churches, carrying the tools, which were scarce in those days, backwards and forwards from one church to the other, to aid the workmen.

At Guéméné, a little town on the river Scorff, we are still in the interior of the country. It is in some ways more civilised than Le Faouet, but as far removed from railways, and with as little communication with the outer world.

M 2

Let us first give our experiences of the principal inn, which is on the left, looking up the street in the sketch, where travellers are driven under an archway into a wide stable-yard, and enter the house by the kitchen. The beds are clean and comfortable enough, the fare is homely but plentiful, and there is nothing to scare away the most fastidious. At the midday meal we have trout, caught a little way down the river Scorff, one or two dishes of meat, an omelette if desired, and, as usual, very good bread, butter, and cider. The

dinner, or evening meal, is rather more elaborate, especially if a fresh traveller has come in. The view, across the table at breakfast time, of the presiding genius of the inn, the bottle of cider, the large wineglass, and the half cut loaf, are all depicted exactly. The vacant chair is soon to be occupied by a commercial traveller, who has been busy all the morning in the town, doing more havoc in the one day that he devotes to Guéméné than we like to think of. He represents a cheap clothier's house at L'Orient, and has tempted many of the quiet inhabitants to change their simple stuffs and white caps for the more fashionable dresses and hats of the town. It should be

remembered, however, that it is to this very *commis voyageur*, whom
we travellers are apt to treat with scant courtesy and whose pro-
ceedings we often regard with anything but pleasure, that we owe
the comforts of these inns, and the possibility of travel in remote
places. The commercial traveller, coming from Vannes or L'Orien

is the pioneer in such towns as Guéméné; he teaches the Breton
innkeeper the mysteries of civilised life, and the art of living
differently from the lower animals. It is a heavy penalty to pay,
from the artistic point of view, that he should bring his patterns and
his sham jewellery, and leave so much of it behind in Guéméné.
But our little waiting-maid is not yet converted to the policy of
adopting modern ways. Her spotless white cap and sleeves, neat

dress, and rows of pendent coins, are of a pattern as old and characteristic as the gables of the houses of Guéméné.

So bright and charming is our little maid this morning that it is
difficult to believe that she came out of a carved wooden bedstead
let into the wall of the kitchen (a bed of two stories, holding four!),
that she does most of the work of the hotel, and helps in the stable.
It is enough for us to record that travellers are well cared for: that

Englishmen come here for the fishing, and sometimes stay for weeks,
living at the rate of four or five francs a day, including everything.

The streets of Guéméné are full of people on Sunday morning—men
in short jackets, wide trousers, and black, broad-brimmed hats, old
women in the comfortable *coiffe* sketched above, girls with white caps and
stomachers, short dresses, and neat shoes, all coming into the church and
afterwards meeting in the street. These are principally country people;
but the inhabitant of Guéméné, the small *propriétaire* or *employé*, who
lives in the town, often wears a semi-nautical attire, as sketched overleaf.

Five old women sit together in the road, their chairs drawn
together for company, and to make an inclosure for two or three
little tottering inhabitants of Guéméné, who at the age of three are
dressed in the costume of their ancestors. Here the harmony of
costume and architecture, both in form and colour, strikes the eye at
once, and we want nothing to complete the picture. There is
nothing, it seems, to add, nothing to leave out; let us stay for a month

(we are inclined to say) and sketch in the high-street of Guéméné
such figures as are standing talking together at an old-fashioned
doorway, opposite to our inn. But the scene soon changes, and out
of one of the old houses, dark in the interior, with a floor below the
level of the street, comes a lady with a nurse and child; she has a
light dress with a train, a hat with scarlet feathers, and a parasol.
She is going for a promenade, and, as she passes down the street, is
greeted by the old women thus: "See they carry their tails in their
hands, these fine demoiselles!"

The Café du Nord is a favourite house of call, and thither the men resort to play at cards or billiards, whilst the women bring out their chairs and sit under the eaves, knitting, gossiping, and watching the passers-by.

There is no traffic in the streets, and no fear of being disturbed. A newspaper may arrive in the evening to inform the inhabitants of the last market prices, or that a workman has fallen out of a window

in Paris. A very few items of local intelligence suffice for Guéméné,
which is too much occupied with its own interests to care for what

the rest of the world calls news. The sun and moon rise and set for Guéméné alone ; it is the "boss" of *their* wheel of life.

We have seen only the high-street of Guéméné, but the town should be viewed from above, with its grey roofs, its church tower, and the ruins of a castle eight hundred years old, in the midst of beautiful hills, bright with gorse, and grey with granite boulders : and a view reaching far away over a wooded valley with the river Scorff winding towards the sea.

On one evening there is a great gathering at the old café with high-pitched roof, at the division of the two streets at the top of the sketch on page 165. The daughter of the popular hostess has been betrothed at the presbytery, and in a month she is to be married. She has her *dot*, or portion, of a few hundred francs, and her husband that is to be, his little farm ; they have met to celebrate the occasion, and their immediate friends make merry until far into the night. They all sit together round a rough table in the little room, the lamps lighting the girls' faces, the men in blouses or white jackets, with bright buttons ; a background of timbered ceiling, smoke, laughter, songs, and jollity, continued long after the lights go out in the street and the moon rises over the valley. All will go well with them if the bottle which first drew them together does not scatter their happiness too soon.

CHAPTER XII.

STE. ANNE D'AURAY — CARNAC — LOCMARIAKER.

ON the 24th of July we take up our quarters at the comfortable Hôtel Pavillon d'en Haut, at Auray. To-morrow is the great day of the Pardon of Ste. Anne, the occasion of the annual pilgrimage to the miraculous well, whither from far and near, on foot and on horseback, in carts and other strange road conveyances, and by excursion trains, come pilgrims to the shrine of Ste. Anne. Like the great annual gatherings at Guingamp and at Ste. Anne la Palue, of which we have spoken, the Pardon of Ste. Anne attracts a strange medley of people, and thus it is that the ordinarily quiet little town of Auray, situated four miles from the shrine, is crowded to overflowing.

The town of Auray, which contains about 5000 inhabitants, is finely situated above the river which bears its name. It was formerly a port of commercial importance, but its trade has drifted to Vannes and L'Orient, and it is best known to travellers as a starting-point for visiting the fields of Carnac and Locmariaker; also as a pleasant and healthy place of residence, where fishing and shooting can be obtained. There are no objects of great antiquity to be seen at Auray itself, its historic castle has disappeared, but there is much to interest the traveller in the old streets with timbered houses, leading down to the river.

On a wide *Place* a few yards off, called the Belvédère, is a column
to ascend to see the view, looking northward and eastward, in the
direction of Vannes, over a wide stretch of cultivated land, pastures,
and woods, dotted with white houses and church spires, one of which
is Ste. Anne d'Auray.   Immediately beneath is a rocky, precipitous
path down to the river, with small vessels loading and unloading, and

the grey roofs of toy-like houses and warehouses on the quay.   A
sudden cloud of smoke, which curls through the gorse and bushes
which conceal the greater part of the river from view, comes from
a little steamer which has arrived from Belle-Île with the evening
tide, and has brought another crowd of pilgrims for Ste. Anne.   All
is quiet and beautiful from this vantage-ground ; the air is soft, and
slowly waves the tree-tops in the avenue which skirts the Belvédère
on its southern side ; there is nothing to indicate the tumult of to-
morrow.

The morning of the 25th of July is bright, and the gilt statue of Ste. Anne glitters above the trees. If at this moment we could look down from the spire of its church, upon the country round, we should see on every road, and across the open land, little dark specks which are pilgrims all tending one way—to the shrine. They have been coming all through the night, camping in the fields and sleeping at the roadside. The broad Roman road from Vannes is covered with carts and carriages, and more people are arriving by the river.

FALLING ON THE BELVÉDÈRE, AURAY.

The crowd that has assembled in the open square near the church of Ste. Anne at six in the morning numbers several thousands, and increases every hour. They are pilgrims of every grade, from the marquis and his family, who have driven from Vannes the evening before, and stay comfortably at the large hotel, to the solitary herdsman in goatskin coat and wooden shoes stuffed with straw, who has walked for two days and nights from his home in the Montagnes Noires. But they have come on the same errand, and will stand side by side before an altar in one of the side chapels, and

burn their candles together. They both believe, or are taught to
believe, in a legend that some time in the seventeenth century a saint
appeared to one Nicolazic, who rented a farm near this spot, and
commanded him to dig in a field for her image, and to erect a chapel
to her memory. They both have heard of the miraculous cures at
the well of Ste. Anne, and believe that no household can prosper, no
ships are safe at sea, no cattle or crops can thrive, unless once a year,
at least, they come to burn
candles to Ste. Anne; and
they both have wife, mother,
or sister christened *Anne*,
the name in fact of nearly
every child we see to-day.

The miraculous well of
Ste. Anne is in a large inclosure at the western end
of which is the Scala Santa,
a small, raised chapel, open
to the air and covered by
a cupola; a modern wooden
erection about twenty feet
from the ground, approached
on either side by a covered
flight of steps. It is from
this platform that the opening ceremony of the Pardon
takes place in the afternoon
of the 25th of July, when after a procession round the town with a brass
band and banners, the bishop of Vannes, or other dignitary, addresses
the people in the open square. The procession is a long one, gay
with the green-and-gold-embroidered vestments of the priests, and
bright with the white robes of the acolytes with their crimson sashes;
a quickly moving procession of bareheaded men singing the litany of
Ste. Anne, with banners (representing different departments and com-

munes) waving above them, and silver crosses and relics carried high
in the air. The crowd presses forward to see, and forms a narrow
lane to let them pass to the Scala Santa, where the head of the
procession comes to a standstill, and as many of the priests and
attendants as can crowd on to the steps stand as a sort of bodyguard,
whilst the bishop addresses the multitude assembled in the square
beneath.

Then the outsiders of the crowd get up and watch the pro-

ceedings (including a cook in white cap and apron, who sits upon
the hotel wall), some eagerly from curiosity apparently, some with
devotion, and some, it must be confessed, with an easy, jaunty air
more appropriate to a show in a country fair. There are several
hundreds on the grass before us in the bright sun, in the glare of
which the sketch was taken, sitting together in parties, kneeling in
prayer, or standing close together intent upon the scene.

What those upturned faces were, and what the good bishop saw
beneath him in the crowd, as he rolled forth a discourse full of

earnestness and eloquence, the pencil has recorded in the sketch. It gives, as no words could describe, the mingled expression of feeling on the faces of the pilgrims, and tells more eloquently than any argument that the influence of the Church is on the wane in Brittany. The words spoken are the old story: first the history of "the miracle of Ste. Anne," then an exhortation as to the importance of confession and of works of charity and masses for the dead. The costume of the people that listen is nearly the same as in 1623, when Ste. Anne appeared in a wheat-field to a peasant; and yet—and in spite of all accounts of the earnest devotion of the people—if we look at the aspect of the crowd, we seem to understand the matter better than we ever did before.

They stand bareheaded in the sunshine, old and young, rich and poor; on the left, the pretty *bourgeois'* daughter, from Auray, in plain cloth dress, with velvet body, dark green shawl, and neatest of shoes; behind her, in the background, a contingent from more remote districts, farmers and small traders, the majority being comfortable people who have come by train. The spare old woman with eccentric expression and worn hands, holding purchases, or plunder, in her apron, is not a pauper, but a hanger-on at a large household, who has saved money. Next, nearer to us, is a peasant farmer, with long grey hair, in white jacket and breeches and leathern girdle, who has come on foot from his home in the interior. He has walked all through the night to be present at the Pardon, as he has done every year, going through the round of services and exercises, contributing several francs in money to the church, buying a few charms and trinkets, and then plodding home. Behind him, with stick and umbrella under arm, holding beads in her hand, with fat red face, a white hood and apron, is a comfortable farmer's wife from Baud; on her right an old woman in dark green *coiffe*, framing a screwed-up face, a study of colour in bronze and green. Behind them is a tall, bareheaded man with his daughter, two of the best types of Bretons in the crowd. On the right in the sketch is a pretty figure with a cross on her breast, with shining face, in the white cap and

At the Pardon of Ste. Anne d'Auray.

wide collar so common in Finistère; and, next, three peasants, old
and wrinkled, bronzed with sun and grime, the common type at
Pardons. Thus—leaving out some of the more hideous aspects of
deformity and disease—this sketch gives an exact picture of the crowd,
and a true idea of the strange mixture of curiosity, amusement, and
religious awe with which the celebration of Ste. Anne is received in
the present day.

Let us add a few notes
of the scene on Sunday, the
second day of the Pardon,
when the crowd is greatest,
and when there must be collected at least 10,000 people;
when, besides the peasants
and country people, visitors
from Paris and other parts
of France have filled to overflowing the large modern
hotel, the courtyard of which
is full of carriages and conveyances of all kinds. In the
streets and round the open
square there are booths for
the sale of trinkets and toys,
rosaries, tapers, statuettes, and
medals of Ste. Anne, besides
the more common objects for

sale at a country fair. In the roadway women cook fish and cakes
(*galettes*) at charcoal fires; there are itinerant vendors of gigantic
wax candles, there are peep-shows and other amusements, skittles
and games like quoits, played with leaden counters of the size of a five-
franc piece. There is every kind of amusement in honour of Ste. Anne,
and the family meetings and gatherings, that take place round the cafés
and in the open fields, suggest a picnic more than a pilgrimage.

N

But it is in the street leading to the church door, and in the adjoining cloisters of a convent, that the more serious aspects of the Pardon are to be witnessed, some of which it would be impossible to record in a sketch.

From four o'clock in the morning masses have been said, and in and out of the church there has been a continual stream of people, all in holiday attire, and nearly all wearing strings of beads, crosses, or silver ornaments bearing the image of Ste. Anne. They form in groups on the grass in the centre of the cloistered square, close together, some kneeling, some standing erect, with eyes strained upwards at a cracked and weather-worn statue of the Christ; they tell their beads, and drop sous into a box at the foot of the cross, the poorest contributing something.

They pass round the cloisters in a continual stream, missing nothing set down for them, but stopping and kneeling at each "station" with expressions of devotion and awe at some grotesque paintings on the walls representing the Passion. They stop and pray, some on one knee only with beads in hand, some kneeling low on the pavement, sitting on the heels of their sabots for rest. They have come a long and weary march, they are at the end of their pilgrimage, and so it happens that sitting and praying they fall asleep. A heavy thwack from a neighbour's umbrella falls upon the shoulders of the sleepers, and again they go the round.

By midday the crowd has increased so that movement in the road is difficult. Coming slowly up the narrow street—blocked by carriages, by vendors of "objets de dévotion," and by the crowd that passes up and down—is an, apparently very poor, old man with long dark hair, a white sheepskin jacket and *bragou bras*, a leather girdle and sabots, holding in his hand a hollow candle three feet high; it has cost him six sous, and he will place it presently at the altar in the church with the rest. Following him is a farmer and his wife, well-to-do people, who have come by train, and combine a little marketing with their religious observances. Following them are two young married people with their child, all dressed in the latest costumes of Paris, the father manfully taking off his light-kid gloves, and carrying his candle to the church with the rest.

The scene in the church, where services have been held at intervals all day, and the people crowd to burn candles at the side altars, is of people handing up babies, beads, and trinkets to be blessed; of the flaring of candles, of the movements of tired priests, and the perpetual murmur of prayers.

We have spoken often of the simple, practical, and graceful dress of the women; but here at Auray we must confess that many of the country people in full holiday attire are anything but graceful in appearance. At a side altar of the chapel there is a young face, very fair, with large devotional eyes, deepened in colour and intensity by her white cap; but below it is a stiff, shapeless bodice as hard as wood, and a bundle of lower garments piled one upon the other, till the figure is a rather ungainly sight; her large capable hands hold her book, her rosary, and a stout umbrella; she is encumbered with clothing, but she differs from her modernised sisters in one thing: her dress is not on her mind when she says her prayers. She is on her knees nearly all day at Auray; but, working or praying, half her young life has been spent in this position. In spite of the grotesque element, which is everywhere at Pardons, the sight is often a sad one; sad, especially, to see so many young faces clouded by superstitious awe. The saying would seem to apply to Brittany, that "national piety springs from a fountain of tears."

We have purposely said little of the repulsive side of the spectacle; of the terrible-looking men and women who have come out of their hiding-places to kneel at the shrine and to beg from strangers; who wander about like savages, and are propitiated with beads. Figures strange, weird, and grotesque, the like of which we shall see nowhere else in the world, pass round the cloisters of St. Anne d'Auray for two days in the year.

There is one half-witted man from the sea-coast, evidently soon "going home"; as he drags himself along, the shadows seem to deepen, and the light from human eyes to burn more fiercely in their tenement

Fed with seaweed, thatched with straw, exposed to the wildest winds of the Atlantic, his home little better than a hole in the rocks, what wonder that he comes across the hills once a year to the Pardon of

Ste. Anne for a blessing; that he prays for a land beyond the sea, visioned in his mind by innumerable candles, and paid for in advance through weary years in his Passage to the Cross!

Many of the pilgrims go through other religious observances before leaving Auray, including washing in the well, going step by step up the Scala Santa on their hands and knees; and all—the poorest and most pitiable—leave *something* in the coffers of Ste. Anne.

And so the long day passes, and at last the tide recedes. What if a strong north wind and the running river Auray could bear them away seaward to be seen no more? What if all the wretchedness, dirt, and disease, collected, as if by a miracle, at Ste. Anne for two days, could, by another miracle as great, be swept away for ever!

CARNAC.

Turning southward and westward from Auray, a drive of eight or nine miles across a dreary-looking district, with patches of pasture interspersed with gorse and ferns, and here and there a peasant leading a cow, driving a cart, or digging in the poor soil—on reaching a rising ground, we see before us a wide stretch of open land, grey and monotonous in colour, and beyond, in the far distance, the horizon line of sea. Leaving the carriage-road, about a mile before reaching the village of Carnac, and turning off to the left, we come rather suddenly, as it seems, upon a stubble field strewn with large grey rocks or stones, some of them six or eight feet high, standing on end, upright, or leaning against each other, but the majority lying *pêle-mêle* on the ground, some half buried in the earth, or hidden by gorse or long grass. They are for the most part smooth and time-worn blocks of, apparently unhewn, granite, of all shapes and sizes, some covered with moss and lichen.

Is this, then, the famous field of Carnac, with its "avenues of menhirs," the object of so many pilgrimages, the origin of so many theories, the birthplace of so many legends? The first impression, we need hardly say, is disappointing, and fills the traveller with that feeling of blank dismay which comes upon him on the first sight of the "Court of Lions" at the Alhambra in Spain. But in a little while, looking westward, and tracing a certain .order and method in the position of "the Stones," he begins to realise that by no ordinary forces of nature, but by some unknown hands in past ages, these pillars must have been raised. But how raised, and by whom brought and strewn on this desolate shore? That they were monuments of the dead, or that they mark the spot where burials took place, forming a consecrated ground for the ancient inhabitants of Armorica, is the commonly received opinion. We are told also that these irregular rows of unhewn stone are relics of serpent worship, that they represent serpents' teeth and the waving lines of its body; also that they mark the places of sacrifice of the Druids; bones and ancient remains of human beings having been found to support this theory.

The "menhir," or "long stone of the sun," will suggest the form of monument used in all ages in religious worship, and the "dolmen," or table stone (which we see in the neighbourhood of Locmariaker), consisting of a chamber formed by placing one large flat stone horizontally on two or more upright blocks, points to the theory of a place of sacrifice in Druidical times, or at any rate to a place of burial.* All else seems vague and mysterious, leading men of succeeding ages to surround the scene with legends and traditions. It has been said that "the ancient temples of aboriginal races are generally to be found where nature wears her saddest and most funereal aspect," and certainly Carnac is no exception to the rule.

---

* The forms of the menhir and the dolmen are indicated on the title-page.

It is a summer's day, and the light south wind that comes over the sea, and gently sways the trees inland, here blows up the sand into our faces, and moans between the stones. It is such a wild and dreary place—where, excepting for a farm and an oasis of a few trees, there is no welcome colour presented to the eye—that the mind leans naturally to the mysterious side, and clings rather to legend and tradition than to historic facts; thus we may see in this confused array an army of pagan warriors turned into stone, and cling, like the present inhabitants of Carnac, to the story of the patron saint of their herds and flocks (St. Cornély), who, pursued to the sea by a host of armed men, and finding no means of escape, cursed his pursuers and turned them into stone.

If, by the aid of the map below, we look down upon the fields of

Scale, 1¼ mile.

Carnac, we shall discern a certain order and method in the arrangement of the stones, and carry away a more definite impression. Thus we see the menhirs (or *peulvens*, "pillars of stone," as they would be more accurately described) arranged in three avenues extending from east to west, commencing irregularly at Kerlescant, continuing in a second group called Kermario, and ending abruptly near Carnac. These avenues form the principal groups, but there are two others, one at Erdeven and one at Ste. Barbe, in a north-westerly direction, besides separate menhirs or *peulvens*, scattered about for miles, half buried in the soil or standing in the long grass. It is estimated by old chroniclers that on these fields there once were 12,000 or 15,000 Celtic monuments; at the present time there are not 1000 to be found upon the fields of Carnac, so many having been destroyed or taken away for building or other purposes.

The most prominent object on the field of Carnac is a mound of stones, once a burial-place, on which there is a chapel and a calvary

SKETCH ON THE FIELDS OF CARNAC.

dedicated to St. Michel. Every traveller ascends this mound to obtain a view, on the one side, of the plains of Carnac, and, on the other, of the peninsula of Quiberon and of the distant islands of Belle-Île, Houath, and Hoedic. From the mound we can also see the spot where the ruins of Roman houses and baths have been found. On the right, as we look seaward, is the little village of Carnac close at hand, with its grey spire and cluster of houses, and here and there in the distance are trees, farms, and patches of cultivation. But all looks dreary and wind-blown, even in summer-time and the inhabitants that stop in their work in the fields to stare, or pursue the tourist through the day, have a wild and weary look that is infinitely sad.

In the church of Carnac are some curious relics, and frescoes descriptive of events in the life of St. Cornély, and in a house opposite is a collection of ancient ornaments, weapons, bone implements, and the like, which have been unearthed from time to time, and are now exhibited for a small fee. Visitors to Carnac should make enquiry for the site of recent excavations made by Mr. Miln, a Scotch gentleman who has devoted some years to archæological labours in the neighbourhood.

Descending to the village of Carnac, the traveller finds a comfortable resting-place at the Hôtel des Voyageurs, and a pleasant contrast to the prevailing sadness of the outer world. In this old-fashioned inn a sumptuous breakfast is prepared in summer for visitors; and here assemble, at midday, the more prosperous part of the community, including priests of antiquarian taste, small farmers, traders in fish, travelling merchants, carriage drivers, and others. The kitchen should be seen by all visitors, with its old fireplace and furniture, ancient clock, and comfortable beds: the pleasant faces and homely welcome of the people giving colour and character to the picture. For a few weeks in summer-time, and at the time of the Pardon of Ste. Anne d'Auray, this little inn is a centre of attraction; it is close to the church, where, round its walls in grave procession, peasants still bring their cattle to be cured—kneeling and praying, in the road, for miraculous aid.

IN THE KITCHEN OF THE HÔTEL DES VOYAGEURS AT CARNAC.

Turning to the north-west, about two miles on the road to Erdeven, is Plouharnel, a village somewhat poor in its surroundings, but giving comfortable accommodation to travellers who come to see the dolmen of Corcorro, one of the largest in Brittany. It consists of three chambers, or "allées couvertes," which were opened in 1830 and found

to contain fragments of earthen vessels, and an urn containing ashes, gold necklaces, &c. The enormous slabs which rest upon and project beyond the upright stones, measured originally, it is supposed, about forty-five feet ; the dolmen now measures twenty-four feet by twelve ; it was formerly underground, but now stands in the open moorland.

The landlord of the inn at Plouharnel formed a collection of relics in 1849, including celts of jade and bronze, taken from this and other dolmens in the neighbourhood. It should be noted that these relics belong to a much later period than others found near Locmariaker, some of which are to be seen at the Museum of Antiquities at Vannes.

The second principal excursion from Auray is to LOCMARIAKER and the island of Gâvr Innis. Locmariaker, or "the place of the Virgin Mary," is situated nine miles in a southerly direction from Auray, and the island of Gâvr Innis (Goat Island) is one of a cluster of little islands two miles east of Locmariaker. At the extremity of the peninsula are two large mounds or tumuli, where various implements and relics have been found, pointing to the time of the Roman occupation of Gaul ; and side by side with these, remains of dolmens and menhirs of a much earlier date.

The Montagne de la Fée, a tumulus of stones about thirty feet high, was excavated in 1863, and in the vaulted chamber or grotto were found necklaces, beads, and other ornaments which may be seen in the museum at Vannes. There is a guide who shows the interior to visitors, and points to the hatchet-shaped inscriptions on the stones. In the Mané Lud, the second great tumulus opened in 1863, was found a large chamber, supposed to have been a sepulchre, containing the skeletons of horses' heads, as well as other bones.

After visiting the tumuli, we cross the fields a little way from

Locmariaker, following upon the track of three priests, to see the great fallen menhir, called "Men-er-Groäch," or "Stone of the Fairies." It is as wild and wind-blown here as at Carnac; in every direction, excepting due north, is the sea, and beyond the sea is a strong south-west wind. The sun that shines upon the islands, and light up the colours of the lichen on the rocks out at sea, scarce illumines the foreground; there is no relief upon the low land but mounds of earth covered with long grass and furze, and here and there, half buried in the ground, grey rocks, strewn about as if by some convulsion of nature. There is no trace of man's handling, as far as we can see; nothing to suggest a monument, and nothing, by contrast,

to give an idea of size. But all at once, as we descend a little behind
some clumps of heather, there loom up before us against the sea and
sky the dark rounded sides of two enormous stones, half buried in
the ground, but raised once as history and tradition tell us, in the
form of an obelisk seventy feet high and sixteen feet in diameter!
All is silent but the wind coming through distant pines, scattering the
gorse blossom on the ground, and bending the long grass. There are
rooks floating in the air, and presently there is a flapping of black
garments as three pilgrims appear upon the more distant portion of
the menhir, clambering down its side. It is an undignified contrast,
but valuable to us for the impression of size and grandeur it gives to
the fallen monument.

Two miles off, on the inland sea of Morbihan—approached
easily by boats at certain times of the tide, but often with great
difficulty owing to the currents—is the small island called Gâvr Innis.
This island is about three quarters of a mile in length, and is green
and cultivated, but so difficult is the approach that it is only in
summer-time that there is much communication with the mainland.
On a summer's day a few adventurous tourists come scrambling up
the wet rocks from boats, to visit the tumulus or mound of stones
which has been excavated of late years, and in which there have
been found various Celtic remains and inscriptions. It is, outwardly,
a mound or heap of stones about 300 feet in circumference, and not
more than 30 feet high.

Of the origin, or use, of these tumuli, of which the one on Gâvr Innis is the most remarkable in Brittany, neither antiquaries of the past nor the present owner, M. Closmedene, who lives on the island in summer, can give a satisfactory account. Like the island of Avalon, it sleeps in an atmosphere of romance and mystery; the most searching of modern antiquaries speaking of the "circular and serpent-like waving lines" cut on the stones of Gâvr Innis as "unaccountable," and of the inscriptions as of "unknown meaning."

Here we may pause, wondering no longer at the superstitions of the peasants, or the romances and legends of the people of Morbihan.

CHAPTER XIII.

VANNES.

A FEW miles from Auray and Carnac is the ancient city of VANNES, the chief town of the department of Morbihan and the capital of Basse-Bretagne. This city, from its position, is the natural point of departure for travellers entering Brittany from the east, as it is also the natural place of rest when coming from the west.

There is not much to attract the traveller at first sight, but the result of several visits is to leave an impression of great interest on the mind. One of the oldest, perhaps *the* oldest, of the cities of ancient Armorica, its very name and its position carry us back to early history, when the fleets of the Veneti commanded these seas, and were finally conquered by Cæsar in the sea of Morbihan, their leaders put to death, and their people sold for slaves.

The part of Vannes of most interest to travellers is the old city with its narrow streets and overhanging houses, and the remains of its walls and gates. In the narrowest part, near the Place Henri-Quatre, there rises between the eaves of the houses the square tower and spire of the cathedral of St. Peter, a structure dating from the eleventh century, altered and almost rebuilt in the fifteenth. The interior of the cathedral is gloomy, and the streets which surround it are dark and old. There are some cloisters and a finely sculptured porch of dark stone. The principal chapel in the interior is

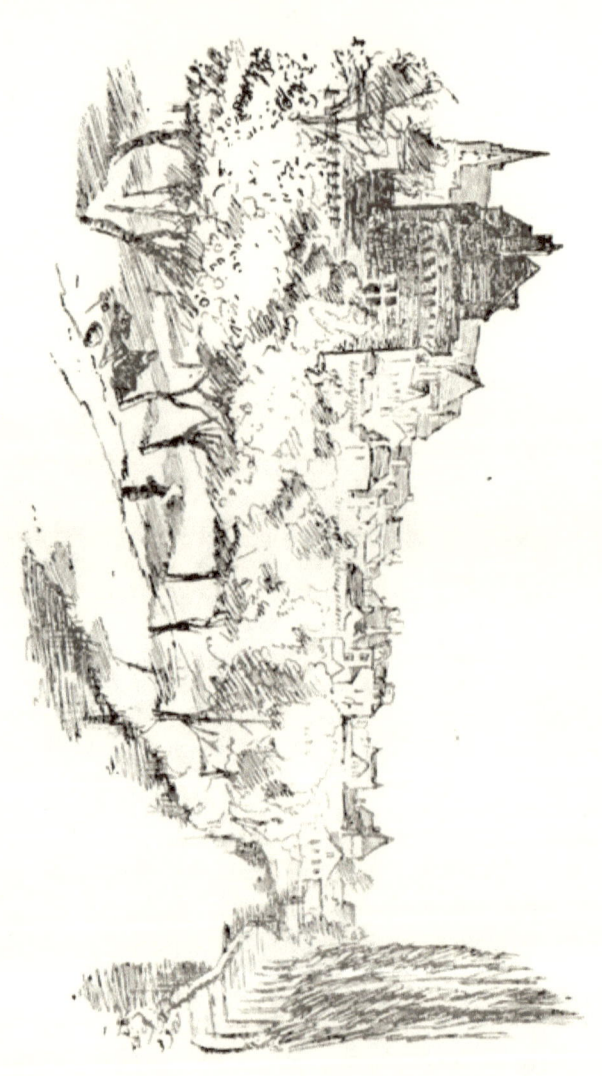

dedicated to the Spanish Dominican monk St. Vincent Ferrier, who evangelised the province in the time of Duke John V., and died at Vannes in 1419. The relics of this saint are once a year carried in procession round the town.

There is one side chapel with an altar, on which are three glass cases, in one of which are relics, and, apparently, some wax models of bones and imitation jewels ; above these, between the folds of a curtain half drawn aside, is a painting of Ste. Marie de Bon Secours, to whom the chapel is dedicated. The light through a narrow stained-glass window falls upon the figure of an old woman, holding beads in her worn hands, who kneels upon the scagliola steps before the altar. There is nothing uncommon in the sight ; but there is a romantic story that this old woman and the beautiful Madonna are one and the same ; that she had sat in her youth as a model for the Holy Virgin, and that she kneels every day before the portrait of her old self.

We have spoken of the cathedral and of its patron saint, because Vannes is an ecclesiastical city of importance, the see of an ancient bishopric, and a radiating point for the church in Morbihan ; but, as a matter of fact, we see and hear very little of the church at Vannes ; and it seems by contrast with the country — where every wayside has its cross or holy fountain, every district its little chapel or altar with saints and relics amongst the trees, every group of peasant-women a pastor—that the country people have more than their share of homilies and exhortations.

Coming from the interior, we miss the attitude of religious awe amongst the women, which seems to be put off at the city gates ; and we miss, also, the individuality of costume which vanishes fast in towns. If we were to picture the people as we see them on Sunday in Vannes, they would be very ordinary indeed, with just a sprinkling of white caps, and a few touches of embroidery on a shawl or a blouse, to remind us that we are in Morbihan ; and in their general attitude they would seem as much at a loss for occupation as in other centres of civilisation where galleries and museums are closed on Sundays.

There is a museum of Celtic antiquities at Vannes, containing a

collection of ornaments, flints, &c., found in the cromlechs at Carnac
and the neighbourhood, which is well worth visiting; and there are
various shows and amusements for the people on the *Place* and in
the public gardens; but the fact remains that the majority of the
working inhabitants sidle off on Sunday morning as we see them in

the sketch, gravitating one by one towards every house outside of
which hangs a bunch of dried mistletoe or broom.

There are many picturesque old houses such as the above; there
is a walk by the river under the old walls and towers, and another
in the upper town with a view far away towards Nantes and the sea;
and there is almost southern warmth and colour under its sunny
walls, where we are sheltered from the winds of the Morbihan.

The people that we see are for the most part pleasant and prosperous-looking, busy in commerce or in agriculture. There is, it is true, more than one regiment of the line quartered here, and the cafés, bright with plate-glass and gilding, are full of warriors of various sizes; in the morning and in the evening the air vibrates with regimental drums, but there is little else to remind us that the inhabitants are the direct descendants of a warlike nation, and that

barons and knights once defended the battlements and towers of Vannes. The morning is spent at billiards in most of the cafés, and in some, especially frequented by the townspeople, there are such groups as the above.

Outside the café, seated on a bench, is a French commercial traveller, dressed like a common dandy from L'Orient, with blue frock-coat, white trousers, very narrow at the bottom, hair cut close to the head, and a portentous moustache; and he does with it what

every human creature seems to do with an artificially contrived tuft
of hair on his upper lip, he twitches it round and round and pulls at
it without ceasing; he has done this every day for many years, and
the action, apparently, relieves his mind. The sight is familiar in
civilised communities, but this figure contrasts so strongly with the
clean-faced, dignified Bretons that it seems time to pack up our sketch-
books and depart.

THREE HOT MEN OF VANNES.

Are the fashions changing in Brittany? or is it only the usual
tourists' cry, the complaint of those who resent all change in costume
and dwellings in order that villages should remain "picturesque," who
look upon their brother living in a hovel as they do upon an
old door-knocker or a china plate? Let us think of the influences
at work in out-of-the-way places, where the travelling *marchand des
bettes*, who has followed us through nearly every village in Brittany

with his caravan of side-spring boots, plies his terrible trade; and let us remember the expression on the faces of the dancers in the booth at Châteauneuf du Faou, at the arrival from Quimper of the "fine lady," who stands up with her relations to dance the gavotte in the latest fashion of the towns.

Before leaving Vannes, we should go down at night to the old Place Henri-Quatre, where the roofs of the houses meet overhead, where, in moonlight, the gables cast wonderful shadows across the square, and above our heads rise the towers of the cathedral with a grandeur of effect not to be seen at any other time, or from any other point of view. It is then that the cathedral precincts look most mysterious in their darkness; narrow, irregular streets with open gutters, lighted only by a glimmer from latticed windows, and where, from old doorways, figures are dimly seen to pass in and out. It is a poor quarter, where a Dutch painter would find work for a lifetime.

We said that there was no light in the streets, but, passing round the cathedral, there is a strong light from a lantern held close to the ground; it is the *chiffonnier* of Vannes (who, like his Parisian *confrère*, has learned the art of pecking and discrimination from the fowls) wandering through the night with his basket and iron wand.

One more note made in Vannes in stormy autumn-time. We go down to the port, sheltered from the wind by a high wall, through which narrow passages have been made to reach the sea. It is nearly dusk, and the rough-hewn edges of the stone wall stand out sharply against the sky. As we pass one of these, facing the west, the narrow opening to the shore is illumined by a blood-red sunset light, so bright by contrast that three figures coming towards us from the seashore step, as it were, out of a furnace. They have men's voices, but as they approach and pass us hurriedly, we see that their heads are bare, and that their robes touch the ground. Upon their shoulders they carry a "dear brother" to his rest—the drift of last night's storm-tide. Next morning a rough stone cottage-door just outside the town is hung round with black—the drapery giving an appearance of height, and almost grandeur of dimensions, to the little interior—and resting upon the step is the projecting end of a wooden coffin painted white. There are candles burning on either side; a metal crucifix is placed on the doorstep, and on a little table on the ground in the road is a vase of flowers. The neighbours pass up and down crossing themselves, and muttering Latin words of prayer for the dead, and the little children stand and stare. Two days after there is a bright procession, headed by a priest and acolytes in white robes, with hymns and incense, followed by a little crowd bareheaded, all struggling against the wind, to a plot of ground on a promontory near the seashore, where the poor Breton is taken to his rest.

There is a crowd of his forefathers here before him, with black wooden crosses where their heads should be; they are planted out in rows, and labelled with wooden sticks to mark their species, and the

garden, is walled in with stones and great rock boulders to keep out
the wind. But it is a dreary place; the wind finds it out from behind
the stones, blows down the wooden crosses, and strews the ground with
seaweed and dead leaves; nothing resists the havoc of the wind over
the graves, but some bright yellow *immortelles* and some metal
images of the Christ.

In the neighbourhood of Vannes there are numerous interesting
excursions to be made, especially southward to the peninsula of
Rhuys, on the south side of the sea of Morbihan, to Sarzeau (where
Lesage, the author of *Gil Blas*, was born), and to the abbey of St.
Gildas, also to the ruins of the fortress of Sucinio, built in 1250
by Duke Jean de Roux. A few miles to the north-west is the
military town of Pontivy, now called Napoléonville, to be reached
easily by railway from Vannes; and near it the village of St.
Nicodème (*see map*), where on the first Saturday in August one of
the largest gatherings of the people takes place. The Pardon of
St. Nicodème is as interesting as any described in this book, but
the customs and ceremonies are too similar to others to be described
without wearying the reader with repetition.

A little farther south, and we should enter the department of the
Loire-Inférieure; we are in fact but a few miles from the city of
Nantes, so well described by Miss Betham-Edwards, in *A Year in
Western France*. In this neighbourhood are the sunny vineyards of
St. Nazaire, the salt districts of Croisic where the costumes of the
inhabitants are again most curious, and the little sea-coast villages
pictured by Mr. Wedmore in his *Pastorals of France;* but there is
enough in the Loire-Inférieure for a separate book, peopled by Breton
folk of an altogether different type.

We have said little of the ancient châteaux of Brittany, many of
which are in good preservation, and are inhabited by direct descendants
of the barons of the fifteenth century; but we would suggest to
the traveller, before leaving Vannes, to visit the picturesque castle of
Elven, where Henry of Richmond, afterwards king of England, was
confined for fifteen years; and, if possible, to go by road to Josselin

where there is one of the finest châteaux of the Renaissance. The numerous sketches, of Breton folk, in this book have prevented us from dwelling more at length on the architectural features of the country, which have been described in many books of travel.

What clings to our recollections of Brittany? Some things that

are not beautiful, and which by no stretch of fancy can be described *en couleur de rose.* The public exhibition of disease and human deformities permitted by the church are sights to which English eyes are unaccustomed, and of which the young and untravelled part of our community have happily little knowledge. But no wise determination to see only the "bright side" of things, no infusion of otto of roses amongst these leaves, can take away the stain that clings to many things in Brittany.

It would seem a consideration of some consequence to the numerous English residents abroad, though we seldom hear it touched upon, that their children must of necessity be brought in contact with so much that is cruel and repulsive. Some may think it salutary and right to see these things; at any rate it is part of the bargain with those who live abroad, and the habits of the people can scarcely be interfered with; but it is a source of wonder to visitors to the principal towns that the residents cannot persuade the authorities to keep more decently their streets and public ways.

We will not dwell upon the cruelty to animals, upon the sights to be witnessed in every market-town, such as tortured calves and half suffocated pigs, because cruelty is everywhere, and we as strangers are helpless in a land where it is not considered a sin to inflict suffering upon animals. It is true that any very flagrant acts can be dealt with by law, but the law is seldom enforced.

What does it matter about *les animaux*? asks the kindest-hearted, most motherly of Breton women, whose children drag live birds through the dust as playthings, and whose husband, if he be of a scientific turn, may perchance keep a grasshopper with a pin through his head, *living*, for days in a glass case!

But our lasting impressions of Brittany are of a people and of a country, interesting for their isolation from the rest of Europe: of a people who are, as has been well said, "dwelling in an heroic past that possibly never existed, consoling the failures of their destiny by beautiful fancies, and throwing a grace over their hard, unhopeful lives with romantic dreams and traditions"; of a people who invest every road and fountain with a holy name—for wherever two roads meet, there is a cross or a sign, and wherever three streams meet, they are called La Trinité;—of a land that stands alone in Western Europe, its rocks unmoved by the shocks of tempest from without, and its manners unpolished by advancing civilisation from within; of a land where men look to the sea as well as to the earth for their harvest, where the plough comes down to the water's edge and the nets of the fishermen are dried upon fig-trees, where laden orchards drop their fruit over weather-worn walls on to the sands, and fish, leaping from the sea, alight sometimes in a field of corn ; of a land brightened for a few weeks in summer with the flower of buckwheat, and coloured with the coral of its stems, where the wind sweeps over waves of grass and grain, and scatters the harvest over the sea.

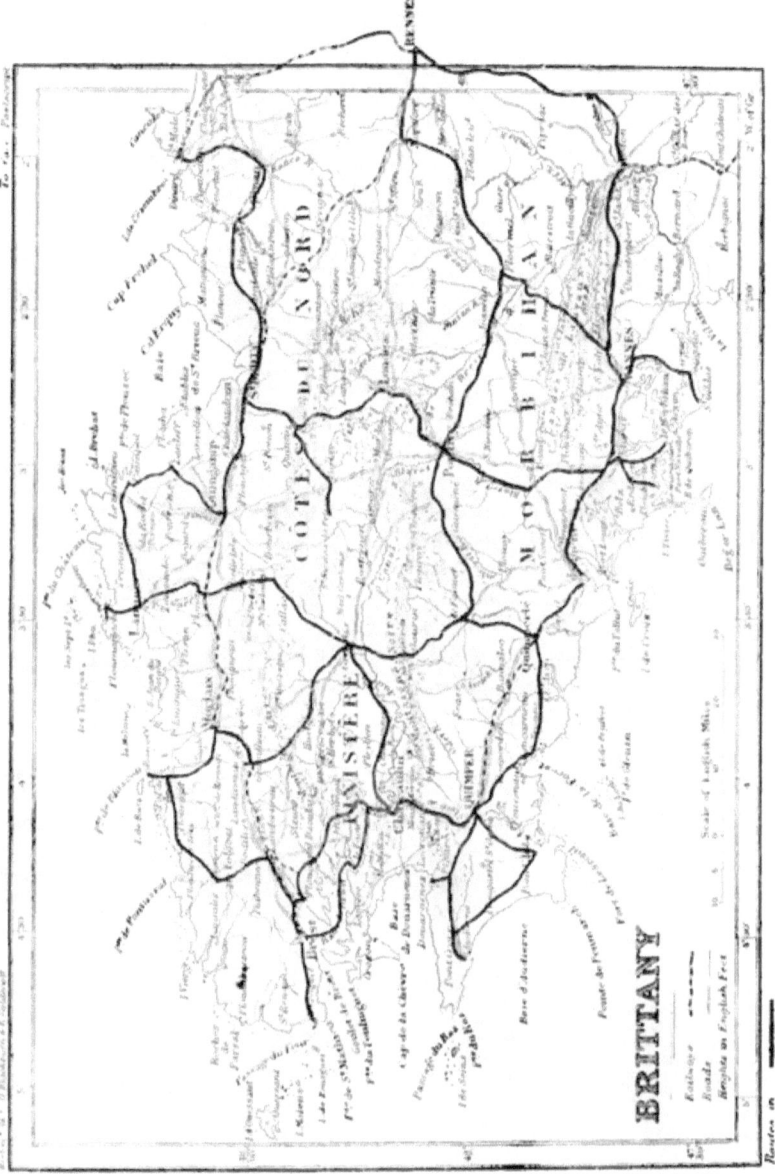

BRITTANY

POSTSCRIPT FOR TRAVELLERS.

The expenses of a journey to and from Brittany and England are limited to a return ticket (£2 12s.) from London to St. Malo, viâ Southampton, which lasts two months. All other travelling expenses on the routes indicated on the map need not exceed five pounds, by taking the public conveyances. Carriages at the usual posting rates. Small and inferior one-horse carriages can be hired nearly everywhere.

The average cost of living at the hotels (which are tolerable in all the towns) is 10 fr. (8s) a day; or by the week, 6 fr. and 7 fr. Pedestrians spend very little anywhere.

The principal rivers for fishing are the Blavet, the Trieux, and the Aven. Anglers should stay at St. Nicolas du Pélem in Côtes-du-Nord, and at Rosporden in Finistère. (See map.)

The most convenient guide-book is the Guide Diamant, by Ad. Joanne, published by Hachette. There is a good road map of Brittany published by Aug. Logerot, 55 Quai des Augustins, Paris.

www.ingramcontent.com/pod-product-compliance
Lightning Source LLC
Chambersburg PA
CBHW030813020726

47499CB00006B/1893